UNDERSTANDING THE ART OF BIBLICAL COUNSELING

Dr. Sabelo Sam Gasela Mhlanga

Copyright © 2023 **Dr. Sabelo Sam Gasela Mhlanga**

All rights reserved. No part of this publication may be reproduced, distributed, or transmitted in any form or by any means, including photocopying, recording, or other electronic or mechanical methods, without the prior written permission of the publisher, except in the case of brief quotations embodied in critical reviews and certain other noncommercial uses permitted by copyright law. For permission requests, write to the publisher, addressed "Attention: Book Rights and Permission," at the address below.

Published in the United States of America

ISBN 978-1-960159-30-4 (SC)

Dr. Sabelo Sam Gasela Mhlanga
222 West 6th Street
Suite 400, San Pedro, CA, 90731
drsamhlanga@gmail.com

Order Information and Rights Permission:

Quantity sales. Special discounts might be available on quantity purchases by corporations, associations, and others. For details, contact the publisher at the address above.

For Book Rights Adaptation and other Rights Permission. Call us at toll-free 1-888-945-8513 or send us an email at admin@stellarliterary.com.

TABLE OF CONTENTS

LIST OF FIGURES
PREFACE v
1 INTRODUCTION 1
    Familiarity with the Literature 4
    Void in the Literature 8
    Thesis Statement 9
2 BIBLICAL AND THEOLOGICAL FOUNDATION
   FOR COUNCELING THOSE WITH HIV/AIDS 10
    Analysis of HIV/AIDS Origin and Stigma 11
    The Church in Response to HIV/AIDS 21
    Practical Response to HIV/AIDS through Biblical Counseling 27
    HIV/AIDS and Leprosy Compared 32
    Embracing HIV/AIDS Positive People in the Church 34
    Conclusion 37
3 SOCIAL RESPONSE TO HIV/AIDS THROUGH BIBLICAL COUNSELING 38
    Counseling HIV/AIDS Church Members to Cope with Stress and Depression 39
    Sexual Behavioral Change of HIV/AIDS Positive Members 44
    Counseling Children with HIV/AIDS 47
    Challenges Women with HIV/AIDS Face 50
    Rational Emotive Therapy as a Model for Interventions 55
    Counseling HIV/AIDS Church Members with Suicidal Thoughts 56
    Counseling HIV/AIDS Orphans 60
    Conclusion 64
4 THEORETICAL AND PRACTICAL RESPONSE TO
   HIV/AIDS THROUGH BIBLICAL COUNSELING 65
    The Value of Knowing One's HIV/AIDS Status 65
    Strategies to Combat HIV/AIDS in Families, Church, and Community 67
    Conclusion 76

5 RESEARCH IMPLICATIONS, APPLICATIONS AND FURTHER RESEARCH 77
    Research Implications 77
    Research Applications 79
    Further Research 81
    Theological Reflection 83
    Personal Reflection 83
    Conclusion 85

BIBLIOGRAPHY 86

LIST OF FIGURES

1. Human Composition
2. Triangular relationship between the family, the church, and Community

PREFACE

Counseling HIV/AIDS positive people in the church has become one of the job descriptions of local church pastors, but it has also become every member's responsibility to respond to those who are infected. It is the most complex and challenging disease of the twenty-first century. In Africa in general and Zimbabwe in particular, it has awakened the church to a greater extent. It is in that context that this thesis was written to examine and investigate the biblical response to HIV/AIDS through biblical counseling. I would like to extend my profound gratitude to my professors, Dr. Michael Wilder, and Coleman Ford who have spent much of their time, resources, and patience to make this thesis possible. My editor, Dr. James Chancellor, did splendid work. I pray that this thesis will benefit Christians, churches, and non-governmental organizations to respond to HIV/AIDS positive people.

My heart-felt thanks to my dear wife, Judith, and our children, Blessing, Shalom, Prosper, Emmanuel, and Joseph-Sam, Jr., who gave me all their support spiritually, socially, and morally. I am grateful to the Southern Baptist Theological Seminary, a great Christian institution that trains and educates minds, nurtures spiritual growth, and empowers and commissions students to fulfill the Great Commission (Matt 28:18-20 NKJV), led by my friend, Dr. R. Albert Mohler who has championed the reformation of SBTS since 1994 for the glory of God. Many thanks also to Dr. Terry Seelow who has been a friend and colleague at St. Matthews Baptist Church as I interned under him for four years. Above all, I am thankful to God the Almighty, for giving me the strength and good health to serve Him and to write this thesis that I pray will help thousands of people, churches, and organizations to respond to HIV/AIDS positive people. To God be the glory, honor, and praise from generations to generations and forever and ever, Amen.

CHAPTER 1

INTRODUCTION

The result of the fall in Eden has brought all kinds of sufferings in human history. Diseases are some of the predicaments that human beings face as a result of sin. Leprosy is a disease that has a similar stigma to HIV/AIDS. The thesis will have a comparative analysis between leprosy and HIV/AIDS, the causes, the social impact, and the stigma of the two diseases. Although no specific texts in the Bible that mention HIV/AIDS, the analysis of the texts in the context of leprosy will highlight the similar stigma of HIV/AIDS that patients face today. This thesis is a comparative case study about the social response in the Old and New Testaments to lepers as it relates to modern AIDS concerns. Gill writes,

It is not possible to find, in the Bible, an exact parallel to stigmatization of those with HIV/AIDS: and yet within the biblical tradition, there are many examples that point to the way in which the stigmatized of the day were treated. We need to learn from the manner in which Jesus related to and responded to the stigmatized, for example, to the lepers, Samaritans, a menstruating woman, and those with physical and emotional disabilities.[1]

The thesis will expound on leprosy in the Bible and its similarities with HIV/AIDS. The church has become a refuge for those who are HIV/AIDS positive as they offer hope and moral support to the infected. After one finds out that he or she is HIV/AIDS positive, society rejects and stigmatizes them. Hoffman contends, HIV disease is not simply a physical entity. Rather, the impact of the disease is reflected in many other important ways, such as in emotional responses, copying strategies, self-image, and changes in life goals. But the physical aspects of the disease often lead to the first awareness that something is amiss; then they become markers of the relentless progression of the disease.[2] Almond concurs with Hoffman that HIV is not simply a physical issue: "AIDS raises a number of ethical and social problems which must inevitably be confronted by the whole community, by people with AIDS and their relatives, and by those professionally involved."[3] It is a physical, moral, and emotional disease; when one is infected with HIV/AIDS, the family, relatives, church, and community all are affected. When the virus destroys the infected person's immune system, the person is prone to various other diseases. Shepherd and Smith propound,

The virus is matter which border by definition between living and nonliving material. They are actually replicable protein matter which exists in a parasitic sense and can survive only as long as their hosts exist. HIV belongs to a class known as retroviruses because its reproduction process involves the virus using its reverse transcriptase enzyme to replicate its RNA into DNA molecules.[4]

> Available HIV/AIDS drugs (antiviral drugs) do not effectively kill the HIV virus, but instead they can only slow down the progression of the disease in the body. Smith alludes to that effect:

The white blood cells that the virus attacks are T4 lymphocytes, monocytes, and macrophages. The invading virus turns the monocytes and macrophages into virus producing factories for the rest of the individual's life but does not significantly damage the cell. Meanwhile, the T4 lymphocytes are systematically killed off over time.[5] When the virus destroys the infected person's immune system, the person is prone to various other diseases. AIDS is a complex disease in which the virus is unpredictable in how it mutates and it continues to change its structure and generic so much that it has been difficult to find a medication that could destroy and eliminates its incubation in the body.

> Avert Organization reports,

The first reported case of AIDS in Zimbabwe occurred in 1985. By the end of the 1980s, around 10% of the adult population was thought to be infected with HIV. This figure rose dramatically in the first half of the 1990s, peaking at 26.5% in 1997. But since this point, the HIV prevalence is thought to have declined, making Zimbabwe one of the first African nations to witness such a trend. According to government figures, the adult prevalence was 23.7 percent in 2001, and fell to 14.3 percent in 2010.[6]

> As cities, churches, and communities grow rapidly, HIV/AIDS infections also spread in an alarming rate. Avert Organization reports,

Despite years of HIV/AIDS education programs in Zimbabwe, there are still misunderstandings about the disease, its' genesis, and its effects on the body. HIV/AIDS increased with poverty in the last decade, as those infected with the disease engaged in prostitution.[7]

The church must have a strategy to respond to the disease. Avert Organization states, "When AIDS first emerged in Zimbabwe, the government was slow to acknowledge the problem and to take appropriate action. Discussion of HIV and AIDS was minimal."[8] The government of Zimbabwe introduced an HIV/AIDS policy and levy to try to curb the spread of HIV/AIDS in the country in 1999. "Efforts to prevent the spread of an HIV in Zimbabwe have been spearheaded by the National AIDS Council (NAC), non-governmental, religious, and academic organizations."[9]

The government of Zimbabwe has been in the forefront to deal with the disease, but the church has lagged behind for some decades. The church should be the salt and light of the world. There are very few books, articles, and documents that have been written by the church to respond to HIV/AIDS in a biblical way. The government and the church have different views as to how to respond to HIV/AIDS:

> The government's main tool for the prevention of an HIV/AIDS is the use of condoms, male circumcision, and abstinence before marriage, prevention programs aimed at behavioral change and the prevention of mother to child transmission which have been instrumental in bringing about a decline in HIV prevalence.[10]

The church has similar methods, but argues that the only solution to this epidemic is abstinence, faithfulness within marriage, behavioral change, righteous lifestyle, and the fear of God. This thesis will pursue that thought of the church and Christian moral principles. It will also advocate for voluntary counseling and testing for HIV/AIDS.

Bread of International Fellowship Baptist has initiated programs in the past five years to meet the challenges of HIV/AIDS under a ministry called 'Hope for All.' The ministry's main function is to care for the orphans of those who die of HIV/AIDS. It trains volunteers, raises funds for school fees of orphans, guides the orphans for vocational training, provides homebased care, and supplies programs for HIV/AIDS prevention.

The thesis seeks to examine the biblical response to HIV/AIDS positive church members through biblical counseling. With the influx of church members being infected, it has become a church crisis, and it is crucial to find a solution to this problem. Twenty years ago, the disease was not yet discovered and the church did not know about it. Now it has come into the church and needs to be addressed, squarely.

It is in this context that there is an urgent need to examine and investigate the biblical response to the disease. The thesis will examine how leprosy in both New and Old Testaments was regarded and how Israelites treated those with leprosy. By standard, prejudice, and stigma, HIV/AIDS is the closest to leprosy. The Bible provides a good case study in comparative analysis between leprosy and HIV/AIDS. Ultimately, Christ reveals how the church should respond to HIV/AIDS positive people in contrast to the Israelites' responses to the lepers. The thesis will make a comparative analysis of how leprosy was regarded and shunned in comparison to HIV/AIDS today.

Familiarity with the Literature

A great amount of literature is written about HIV/AIDS and counseling. There has been vigorous research on this complex disease, HIV/AIDS, and there is a desperate desire to find a cure for prevention of this deadly disease in the twenty-first century.

Numerous books, journals, articles, and magazines are in the market as scientists, physicians, psychologists, anthropologists, historians, theologians, pastors, and counselors wrestle with the quest to find an answer to HIV/AIDS disease.

Lyn Frumkin and John Leonard in *Questions and Answers on AIDS*, give the possible origin of HIV/AIDS, its genesis, its structure, and how it mutates.[11] The book is resourceful as it gives the background and information about where and how HIV/AIDS started and the spread of the virus in the human cells. The book discusses opportunistic infections which began to occur in homosexuals and users of intravenous drugs in United States in 1981. The book will be of great use to the counselors and pastors as they explain to their clients and members of the churches as to how HIV/AIDS originated and how it started to spread. This work has been helpful in understanding the origin of HIV/AIDS.

The *New Bible Commentary* by D. A. Carson et al., provides sound exegesis of the text of Genesis 3:17-19 NKJV. The commentary expounds on the fall of Adam and Eve and how their sin resulted in the suffering of all mankind.[12] The commentary details the origin of sin and its effects on the past, the present and the future. However, in this commentary, they bring in hope through Christ regardless of the fall. It is a powerful commentary with four theologians who put their thoughts and insights together.

Mary Ann Hoffman's work, *Counseling Clients with HIV Disease* is a helpful resource which was written to respond to HIV/AIDS in both biblical and social circles.[13]

A number of ministers and pastors are confronted with this incurable disease and they do not know how to handle it in terms of counseling HIV/AIDS positive members. Mary Hoffman guides the counselor in how to counsel, comfort, and pray with the patients. The book is a helpful resource in guiding the counselor to biblically help HIV/AIDS church members. With the need to help members of the church to understand and to get involved in helping HIV/AIDS positive members, this book is a "must" read book.

Almond points out in *Aids-A Moral Issue* that AIDS/HIV is not only a physical issue but it is a social and moral issue because it affects the family and community, as well as the nation.[14] She outlines the need for the family, church, and community to help HIV/AIDS positive people to move beyond prejudice and stigma. The book is a valuable resource for the churches with members who are HIV/AIDS positive. Almond believes that the church can bring change and champion the counseling of HIV/AIDS positive members and become a powerful ministry of the church to reach out to the community with God's Word. Paul taught that if one part of the body suffers, the whole body is affected (1 Cor 12:26 NKJV). Almond portrays a similar analogy with apostle Paul. She highlights the importance of counseling HIV/AIDS positive people and to embrace them in the church as they face stigmatization in the society. The book is so helpful to teach how the church should response to HIV/AIDS positive members.

Counseling HIV/AIDS positive members of the church is a ministry that is to be nurtured and equip mature church members to be the counselors. William Amos, in

> *When AIDS Comes to the Church*, purports to warn about the coming of HIV/AIDS in the church and finding the ways to combat it. [15]It is a highly recommended book to be in the shelves of the church library. The book has tools to use in counseling HIV/AIDS patients.

AIDS Pastoral Care: An Introduction Guide, was written by Sean Connolly in 1994. This small book was written with the intent of giving pastors a guide to pastoral care and counseling. Although the book does specifically give guidance to counsel HIV/AIDS positive people, it has valuable materials to help pastors counsel any kind of issue that the members of the church may have. The book gives some guidelines on how to help individuals who seek permanent solutions to their problems such as spiritual, moral, social, psychological, or divorce.[16] It is a good resourceful book for pastors and counselors. Connolly is well versed with pastoral care and counseling and has vast experience. The book was written with thoughtful insights about caring and counseling the church members who face challenges. It is a relevant book for this thesis as it discusses caring and counseling church members with HIV/AIDS. It is written simply and it is easy to read and understand.

Musa Wenkosi Dube wrote *The HIV & AIDS Bible* from a practical experience as a woman born in Southern Africa and having been raised in a culture and tradition that gives women lower position than men. She writes with a mission to send a powerful message about women's predicaments and how they suffer the humiliation of womanhood because of culture and tradition. *The HIV & AIDS Bible*, written in 2008, spells out how women in Africa are infected with HIV/AIDS through their spouses who might have multiple partners. The majority of men in Africa work in the cities to fend for their families and return home after several months. Most of them live with other women during that time and when they return home, they transmit HIV/AIDS to their wives. [17]In the book, Dube wrestles with AIDS and the Bible to determine if the Bible has the answer to AIDS. Although I do not agree with some of her theological debates and conclusions, the book has valuable information about AIDS and the Bible, African women and orphans that are exposed to HIV/AIDS because of the African culture and tradition. The culture and tradition honor men highly in the expense of women and children, thus leave them vulnerable to HIV/AIDS. Her plea and suggestions to revisit African culture and tradition stands out as available information for African scholars to pursue.

In *Counseling the Chemically Dependent: Theory and Practice*, George L. Ricky brings in a different dimension on how to respond to those who are chemically dependent. He highlights the reasons to counsel such people and how to prevent them from addiction. Although the book does not specifically address HIV/AIDS patients, it is relevant to those who are HIV/AIDS positive because they are given a lot of antiviral drugs to decrease the multiplications of the virus in the blood. As the antiviral drugs are prescribed to be taken regularly, their bodies tend to become addicted and chemically dependent. George's book answers the question of how to control drug addiction and gives guidance to counsel the chemically dependent. The book is highly recommended to be read by all counselors to learn how to counsel the chemically dependent and also when to refer clients to other specialists.

Robert D. Enright and Richard P. Fitzgibbons in their book, *Helping Clients Forgive: An Empirical Guide for Resolving Anger and Restoring Hope*, points out the importance of helping clients to forgive and resolve anger and restore hope.[18] The book was written in 2000 with the aim of helping counselors with techniques to counsel people and to learn how to forgive. The book has deep insights and thoughtful ideas to forgive. It is an empirical guide for resolving anger and restoring hope. The book is relevant in the thesis to guide clients to the reason to forgive. Many times, HIV/AIDS positive people shift blame to someone whom he/she suspect could have infected him/her with HIV/AIDS. Although it may be true that someone may have infected him/her with HIV/AIDS, they go through stress and depression. The book has helpful information and is a detailed guide to counsel clients and follow through the process in order to forgive.

In *Stress, Coping, and Depression*, Sheri L. Johnson et al., found it imperative to write about stress, coping, and depression, which are issues of many patients, especially when they find out that they are HIV/AIDS positive.[19] With their practical experience of counseling, Johnson, Field, and Schneiderman help counselors lead the counselees to know how to deal with stress and depression. The book is valuable and helpful in this thesis as it addresses stress and depression. This book teaches how to deal with stress and depression. It is relevant and has biblical counseling guidelines for the purposes of counseling HIV/AIDS.

Many churches, especially in Africa, do not have a counseling ministry because it is regarded as part of the pastor's job descriptions. The counseling, for that matter, was mainly for pre- counseling for a wedding. The second counseling known in the church was when a couple was contemplating to divorce. These are the main issues that merited counseling. As churches grow and different issues crop in, the church has seen the sprint of counseling. Written in 1993, Patricia L. Hoffman's *AIDS and the Sleeping Church* attempted to awaken the church which was in slumber. [20]The book was a wake-up call for the church to take its rightful position and to be prophetic. HIV/AIDS was creeping in the church and the church was still in the denial stage. Hoffman's book is a resourceful book for counseling HIV/AIDS to inform the church about the disease. The book has relevant information to the thesis.

Ronald W. Maris, Alan L. Berman, and Morton Silverman in their book, *Comprehensive Textbook of Suicidology*, was written in 2000 to help clients with suicidal thoughts.[21] HIV/AIDS positive people face many challenges and sometimes contemplate suicide to ease the pain they are going through. The book was written with deep thoughts about counseling those who have given up in life because they are terminally ill, addicted to drug, or experienced divorce or disappointments. The three counselors provide helpful insight on counseling people who have given up and want to die. Although they do not write specifically about those who are HIV/AIDS positive, they outline procedures counselors should follow in counseling sessions. While the book is written with all kinds of patients in mind for professional counseling, the book has vast and useful information for biblical counseling for HIV/AIDS.

Robert J. Perelli's book titled, *Ministry to Persons with AIDS: A Family Systems Approach*, written in 1991, has helped many pastors and counselors across the world to counsel children with HIV/AIDS.[22] The book outlines the approach counselors should use to reach out and counsel children who have been infected by HIV/AIDS through breastfeeding, in rape cases, through blood transfusion and unprotected sex. It is a powerful book that gives pastors and counselors the edge to start the process of counseling parents or family members on how to build trust and good relationships. Stressed relationships aggravate and divert the focus on the disease and promote family disputes. Perelli, in this book brings fresh and mature discussion about these issues. The book contributes to the thesis to minister to people with AIDS and promotion of family unity. Danai Papdatou and Costa Papadatos discuss the predicament of children facing death in their book, *Children and Death*, written in 1991. [23]Children are the center of many families and when they become sick with terminal illness such as AIDS or cancer, their lives are devastated and they do not know what to do next. Papdatou and Papadatos bring in useful information as to how to have a plan in counseling and helping the family to prepare for a child's death. Although it is difficult and challenging to bring the subject to the parents of the children or family members, Papdatou and Papadatos make it easy to understand and to have a plan for counseling them. It is at this time that hope in Christ is ushered about life after death. The child who is facing death can be assured life after death and why he/she should believe in Christ for eternity. It is a resourceful and highly recommended book for every family to have. It contributes to the thesis in many ways including the plan that is highlighted to counsel both the dying children and their families.

Sexual behavioral change can influence the prevention and the spread of HIV/AIDS infections. Promiscuity, sex before marriage, adultery, unprotected sex, and ungodliness has catapulted the spread of HIV/AIDS in Africa in general and in Zimbabwe in particular. Nathaniel McConaghy wrote *Sexual Behavior: Problems and Management* in 1993 in which he spells out the sexual behavior of human beings that has increased HIV/AIDS infections and the spread of HIV/AIDS.[24] He suggests that sexual behavior can be controlled and managed by an individual if he/she wants to change from being promiscuous to a sexual normal human being. Sexual behavior can be controlled, which can reduce the infection and spread of HIV/AIDS. The book is a helpful resource for the thesis and for teaching church members to be sexually responsible.

Void in the Literature

Biblical counseling has not been seen as a vibrant ministry of the church in the past two or three decades, however, recently it has been recognized as a useful entity and ministry to give help to those who are in need. In Ephesians 4:11 KJV, the apostle Paul writes,

> It was he who gave some to be apostles, some to be prophets, some to be evangelists, and some to be pastors and teachers, to prepare God's people for works of service, so that the body of Christ may be built up until we all reach unity in the faith and in the knowledge of the son of God and become mature, at attaining to the whole measure of the fullness of Christ.

Counseling is not mentioned in the list of the gifts given to edify the church, therefore, it is not one of the ministries of the church. In contrary to that argument, they are all embedded in Christ and Paul's teachings in the Gospels and Pauline Epistles.

While they are volumes of literature in print today on biblical counseling, they are not written directly as the biblical response to HIV/AIDS. Books that have been written on HIV/AIDS do not address and give biblical solutions to those who are suffering and dying from AIDS. Letty M. Russell's *The Church with AIDS: Renewal in the Midst of Crisis* is the urgent call for the church to wake up and confront the deadly disease by counseling and teaching about the HIV/AIDS prevention and curb the spread of the disease. The book provides the compelling research that is needed to respond to HIV/AIDS biblically: "We are all living with AIDS, both as a worldwide health crisis and every community and church. Yet many churches still ignore this reality and practice a conspiracy of silence and rejection."[25] One of the biggest challenges of the churches is indifference about HIV/AIDS. No books have been written specifically to biblically respond to HIV/AIDS. No churches in Zimbabwe have set up training centers within the church to counsel HIV/AIDS members of the church. HIV/AIDS positive church members are always referred to get counseling in the clinics, hospitals, or in professional counseling centers.

Robin Gill's *Reflecting Theologically on AIDS, A Global Change* is resource book that fills the gap on the biblical response to HIV/AIDS.[26] Reflecting theologically on AIDS has been a challenge to the church. Most churches still shun, reject, and deny the existence of HIV/AIDS. This book gives insights on why the church should be in a position to devise programs to deal with HIV/AIDS. HIV/AIDS exists everywhere in the world and the church must be in the forefront to deal with it. The church should not wait to be over taken by the world in confronting this deadly disease. Another work that is valuable to bridge the gap of literature is *AIDS and the Sleeping Church*, by Patricia L. Hoffman, which calls the church to wake up from its slump. The book is helpful in highlighting the importance of counseling HIV/AIDS with Christ in mind, which was compassionate and loved every human being.

Thesis Statement

HIV/AIDS is related to the issue of leprosy in Scripture, and therefore, a biblical and theological understanding of care for lepers should serve as a paradigm for counseling HIVAIDS victims. A biblical response to HIV/AIDS through biblical counseling is the key to making the church the salt and light of the world. The church must take the leading role in combating the HIV/AIDS scourge by providing counseling, teaching, training leaders, devising HIV/AIDS prevention programs. The thesis will argue on sociological and biblical response to HIV/AIDS as a social, moral, as well as a spiritual issue.

CHAPTER 2

BIBLICAL AND THEOLOGICAL FOUNDATION FOR COUNCELING THOSE WITH HIV/AIDS

This chapter examines the biblical and theological foundations for biblically counseling HIV/AIDS positive patients. All human problems, including diseases like leprosy, HIV/AIDS, cancer etc., are the consequence of the fall of man. In biblical counseling, the Bible is used as a textbook for counseling. It is in this context that this chapter makes a comparative analysis between leprosy and HIV/AIDS and their stigma. Leprosy is the nearest disease to HIV/AIDS disease and they share a similar stigma. The comparison between leprosy and HIV/AIDS enhances understanding of a similar stigma the infected people go through. Second Kings 5:1-14, Leviticus 13:12-13, Luke 17:12-19 NKJV, and Matthew 8:2-3 NKJV are cited to draw the parallel stigma of leprosy to HIV/AIDS in both Old and New Testaments.

Jay Adams writes that biblical counseling is "analyzing a counselee's problems and discovering the Bible's solution to it or implementing that solution in a biblical way when the solution has been reached." [27] Adams continues to say, "First of all, as I have just noted, the biblical solution to a problem is in twofold: Getting out of his difficulties with God and with his neighbor and teaching him how to stay out of them in the future."[28]

Adams defines biblical counseling explicitly in which the counselor finds the biblical solution for the counselee's problems. In the context of biblical counseling, "The Christian counselor, therefore, must see Christ in every passage that he uses and introduce the counselee to Him there." [29] Adams points out the fact that biblical counseling is about taking the Scriptures and applying them to the problems as a solution for the counselee.

Biblical counseling has become an answer to the church for equipping ministers, counselors, pastors, and church leaders. Adams asserts,

> To put it simply, scriptural counseling is counseling that is wholly scriptural. The Christian counselor uses Scriptures as the sole guide for both counselor and counselee... . Like every faithful preacher of the Word, he acknowledges the

Scriptures to be the only source of divine authority and therefore, judges all matters by the teaching of the Scriptures.[30]

Adams adds, "While all sorts of other resources may be useful illustratively and in other secondary ways, the basic principles for the practice of counseling are all given in the Bible."[31]

The scope of HIV/AIDS shows that HIV/AIDS has caused intense suffering, especially to those who are infected and affected by it. The counselor must know and understand the objectives of counseling. Adams explains,

The counselor must know the purpose of the passage; that is, he must know what God intended to do to the reader (warn, encourage, motivate, etc.) with those words. Then, he must make God's purpose his own in the application of the passage of human needs. But to do this he must develop an exegetical conscience by which he determines never to use a passage for any purpose other than that purpose.[32]

Analysis of HIV/AIDS Origin and Stigma

The origin of HIV/AIDS has been a mystery since it was discovered. Although there have been many theories of its origin, these hypotheses cannot be substantiated in record. Scientists do not know how the AIDS virus came into existence and where it first appeared in human history. Lyn Robert Frumkin and John Martin Leonard assert,

An AIDS-like virus causing Simian Acquired Immunodeficiency Syndrome in monkeys has been isolated. A different retrovirus related to HIV has been isolated recently from wild Africa has found cases of unexplained opportunistic infections in patients as early as 1975, that today would meet the current CDC definition of AIDS. It seems likely that the current epidemic may have first occurred somewhere in Central Africa in the mid-1970s.[33]

The claim cannot be proved however, some scientists speculate that AIDS first appeared in America among homosexuals:

In mid-1981, usual opportunistic infections began to occur in homosexuals and users of intravenous drugs in United States. The infections proved to be uniformly fatal and unprecedented in severity in these previously healthy individuals. This apparently new condition was named the Acquired Immunodeficiency Syndrome, or AIDS.[34]

Old Testament

In God's judgment on the man, Genesis 3:17-19 KJV, reads, "Cursed is the ground because of you," which is the present condition of the land as a result of man's disobedience and rebellion against God. Sailhamer writes,

Verse 18 shows the reversal of the condition of the 'land' before and after the fall. The next verse (19) reverses humankind's condition. Before the fall, man was created from the ground and given the 'breath of life' (2.7). As a result of the fall, human kind must return to the ground and the soil (dust) from which they were taken (3:19). In these reverses, the author suggests that the death sentence (2:17) has now fallen over to God's good creation.[35]

The innocence and the harmony of Eden was distorted and ruined by sin: "The mistakes of Adam and Eve are typical of all sins, but as they were parents of the whole human race their deeds had the gravest consequences…. The long-term effects of sin started to appear."[36] The source of all suffering among humanity goes back to the fall and the consequences of sin (Gen 3:17 -19 KJV). The source of sin and the results of imperfection came after Adam's disobedience.

However, the consequence of sin is redeemed through Christ rather than removed through works. Reno explains, "Thus, to reverse the punishment of men and women requires breaking the bonds of our perverse loyalty to Satan's lies, the belief that the natural conditions of life can fulfill and satisfy. Salvation does criminate or destroys those natural conditions."[37] Johnson asserts,

According to the Bible, the most important soul-healing event of all time was the death and resurrection of Christ, an event that has many ramifications for the soul. The most important outcome was that Christ's death propitiated the wrath of God against sinners (2 Cor 5), which in turn made it possible for God to be the believer's soul healer, Father and friend, all roles that bring comfort and create unique forms of religious coping for the Christian.[38]

Second Kings 5:1-14: Naaman's Leprosy Second Kings 5:1-14 discusses the Syrian army commander Naaman who had leprosy. He was advised by the captive girl from Israel to seek help from the prophet Elisha. He listened to the advice of the young girl, to his servants, and to the prophet, Elisha. He was healed from leprosy. Naaman sought healing by listening to the advice of a captive girl from Israel. Through the wise counsel of the girl, Naaman was healed by following the instructions to dip himself into the Jordan River seven times as he was advised by Elisha.

The description of Naaman's healing entails that God is a merciful and loving God if one comes to Him in humility. Naaman received healing regardless of where he came from. God does not discriminate on the basis of the prejudice that people assign, but acts with His kindness, love, and for a purpose.

Leviticus 13:12-13: Restoration of Unclean Lepers into the Society

> The priests were responsible to examine and determine if the lepers were fit to be among the rest of the Israelites. If the lepers' skins had developed into leprosy, they were forced to move out of the camp. It was atrocious experience. However, if they were healed by any means, they were restored back to the society.

> Liethart points out,

Old Testament leprosy is not Hanson's Disease, the modern form of leprosy that causes limbs to rot and fall off. Instead, it is closer to psoriasis, and its symptoms included flaking skin, discoloration of bodily hair, and exposure of the flesh through the skin (Lev. 13). It is not so much a physical as a symbolic disability, a condition that excludes the leper from the presence of God. [39]

> The account in Leviticus 13:12-13 NIV, illustrates how the lepers were treated in Israel. When people were found to have leprosy, they were thrown outside the camp to die or to recover on their own without mercy from anyone. George Arthur Buttrick writes,

If a man has a swelling, eruption, or bright spot which shows signs of being leprosy, the priest shall diagnose it as such, provided that the hair on the "mark" or "stroke" which looks leprous turns white, and this mark may be sunk in the skin. If there is no such turning white of the hair or sinking of the supposed mark, the man shall be in quarantine for a fortnight, and then, if all is well, be pronounced clean.... If at the end of the fortnight the eruption has spread, the priest shall pronounce it leprosy.[40]

The priests played an important role as far as determining the spread or healing of the leprosy. They were the representatives of the camp of Israel. The Bible clearly spells out that incurable diseases are caused by the sin of men. The priests were responsible for examining the skin of the lepers in order to determine whether it had changed. They had expertise in recommending the lepers to be sent out of the camp in fear of spreading the disease. In the process, they would offer counsel and advice, one would think. What the lepers went through during the examination was traumatic experience:

> The person with such an infectious disease must wear torn clothes, let his hair be unkempt, cover the lower part of his face and cry out, "Unclean!" As long as he has the infection he remains un-clean. He must live alone; he must live outside the camp. (Lev 13:45-46 NIV).

Isolation and stigmatization were designed for public display as a sign of mourning for lepers. Rooker asserts,

> To be outside the camp (the area around tabernacle and courtyard) was considered to be separated from God ... because the presence of God was in the camp. Being outside of the camp parallels the expulsion of Adam and Eve from the garden in Genesis 3 NKJV. [41]

The same philosophy of the Israelites is reflected in today's society in regard to the stigmatization and isolation of HIV/AIDS positive people. One would conjecture similar treatments because the two diseases were/are regarded as a disgrace in the public eye.

Both have similar stigma. Richard Vinson notes,

> Leprosy is described in (Leviticus 13) in some detail, so that the priests can correctly identify it: a white rash or swelling or boil that spreads, especially if it turns the body hair white, with or without itching. Leviticus does not attempt to address the cause of the disease; although there are instances of leprosy being a curse or a punishment.[42]

> The skin of the person with leprosy turns white from head to foot. Hartely asserts, "The priests clear his status in the cultic community by pronouncing him clean. The reason a person with such condition remains clean is that there are no open, i.e., raw, sores, nor is there any involvement beneath the skin's surface."[43] If a person has white skin from head to foot without open sores, he does not have leprosy. Even if the person has not developed leprosy, the person is isolated until he is declared clean by the priest. In the same manner, even if the person has not developed AIDS, the person is stigmatized and usually isolated from the church and society.[44]

> Wenham suggests, "Thus, any very extensive skin disease which entailed peeling of the skin, such as exfoliative dermatitis or, again, exfoliative stage of scarlet fever, was not biblical leprosy." To have leprosy in Israel was a curse and defilement. Buttrick explains, "To the natural repulsion which it evokes there was added for the Jew the sense that it was a defilement of the law."[45]

The community shunned such people and cast them outside the camp until they were proven to be clean by priests. They suffered through humiliation and isolation. They were quarantined. They lived outside the camp and were left to die outside. They were characterized by the stigma because of the nature of the disease. House contends, as lepers they had to live outside the city (Lev 13:46), but they stayed near the gate to beg for food. Ironically, just as the once-leprous Naaman led Syria to many victories over Israel, so now these lepers will lead Israel's looting of Syria's army.... God caused them to hear yet another unseen army (2 Kings 6:17).[46]

The HIV/AIDS stigma is similar to that of Israel toward the lepers who lived outside the city because of their condition. They suffered humiliation, rejection, scorn, discrimination, and isolation.

Second Kings 7:3-20: Four Lepers

The four lepers mentioned in 2 Kings 7:3-20 NKJV show the stigmatization in Israel. The four lepers were at the entrance of the city gate and they decided to go to the city of the Arameans. While on their journey to surrender, the Lord caused the Arameans to hear the sound of chariots and horses and a great army, so they fled, leaving all their possessions. The lepers went in and took as much possessions as they could. They also informed other Israelites in the camp about the good news. The text teaches about those who are rejected from the society but who can bring hope in the camp. The lepers suffered stigma and isolation, similar to HIV/AIDS victims. Blomberg asserts, "Lepers were ostracized from society and lived in 'colonies.' They still exist in many parts of the world today, but the closest counter-parts who most people are familiar may be AIDS victims."[47] The two diseases strike similar stigma and to some extent, isolation as well.

New Testament

In the New Testament, one encounters individuals and groups of lepers who suffered. In the New Testament, Jesus addresses leprosy and its stigma, headlong. He puts things into the right perspective about what to do with people with leprosy. Leprosy is still in existence today but in lower magnitude.

Luke 17:12-19: Jesus Responds to Ten Lepers

Jesus encountered ten lepers as he was travelling to Jerusalem along the border between Samaria and Galilee. As Jesus approached a village, ten lepers met him. As a custom, they stood a distance and called out to him with a loud voice, "Jesus, Master, have pity on us!" Jesus' response was simple: "Go, show yourselves to the priests," (Luke 17:13-14 NIV). On their way, they were healed. Jesus showed compassion to all who needed his service. He did not discriminate. He welcomed sinners to himself and healed the sick.

Buttrick writes, "The compassion of Jesus is once more evident. The sight of a colony of lepers-hands and feet gone, faces marred by gray death-was common enough, and most men grew accustomed to it."[48] Jesus' compassion was unconditional. When they saw that they were healed, one of the ten lepers gave gratitude to Jesus but the other nine did not give thanks. Jesus healed them all in the same way, but the one who came back to thank Christ was also forgiven of his sins. Craddock explains,

> That is, Jesus treats the lepers as already healed, and in their act of obedient faith their healing takes place.... The man is a Samaritan and hence a social outcast and a religious heretic, and has leprosy. But in leper colonies, the common problem renders Jew/Gentile distinctions unimportant and not only on leper colonies; but also in the presence of Jesus.[49]

Jesus demonstrates the love he has for all kinds of people and shows the church how they should biblically respond to the people's needs.

Plummer explains that the Israelites practiced some of these laws which were not written but were practiced by tradition: "The precise distance to be kept was not fixed by law, but by tradition, and the statements about it vary... . They took the initiative."[50] The lepers took the initiative to call on Jesus. In the context of the Jewish tradition, not by law, they kept the lepers outside of the camp. The law does not allow discrimination against people with HIV/AIDS, but people isolate HIV/AIDS victims in society today.

Luke does not identify the nationalities of the ten lepers until in Luke 17:16 NKJV, where he mentions they were Jews and Samaritans. Luke 17:12 tells that per tradition, lepers stood a distance from Jesus and were required to stay outside a resident area. When HIV/AIDS was first discovered in Zimbabwe, infected persons were quarantined to a separate area or hut to avoid contact with (clean) people just as it happened in Israel with the lepers.

> The ten lepers were living outside the camp as the law required. They addressed Jesus as "Master," an ordinary Greek word (*despota* or *epistata*), not using the word "Lord" (*kyrios*). *Didaskolos* is the only title they used to refer to "teacher," not as disciples. Jesus, full of compassion, healed them and they went back to their villages to be examined by their priests, from head to toe, and then were assimilated into the society. The law required segregation of lepers (Lev 13:45-46; Numb 5:2-4 NKJV), and the tradition banned them from mingling with others. Robert H. Stein writes, "The obedience to Jesus' word reveals a certain degree of faith on the part of all ten lepers."[51] The ten lepers had believed what Jesus told them and were on their way to be examined by the priests as the Law required. The interesting part of the story is that these lepers were socially and spiritually outcasts. As Bock puts it, The miracle contained two levels of tension: Samaritans were disliked by Jews, and lepers were shunned by the society in general... . As Jesus continues his journey to Jerusalem, he responds to a cry for mercy. The Samaritan's praise and gratitude in response to God's mercy receives commendation, because exposure to God's grace is good enough, one must receive it. The response of faith to God's grace leads to salvation.[52]

The church, in regard to HIV/AIDS positive people, must respond to a cry for mercy and act just as Christ did. Bock writes,

> Ten lepers intend to speak with Jesus, but they cannot approach him because of their despised disease, (Lev 13:45-46; Numb 5:2-3 NKJV), so they call to him from a distance. Perhaps the closest cultural equivalent to first-century attitudes about leprosy would be current attitudes about AIDS.[53]

>> Society's attitudes toward HIV/AIDS positive people, especially in Africa at the beginning of HIV/AIDS's discovery, was similar to the attitude toward leprosy in Israel, in which those who were infected were despised, rejected, and scorned by society.

In the context of the ten lepers, they cried out for help to Jesus, Jesus responded and the healing occurred out of an act of obedience.

> HIV/AIDS has become an aberration of society and the stigma associated with the epidemic has become a challenge to the church. Like the Samaritans, lepers were culturally isolated, disliked, racial half-breeds and seen as a religious defection. Bock reiterates, "The idea of a Samaritan leper receiving God's help was undoubtedly shocking to many, since they had written off people in either category as being beyond help."[54]

Many times, society and the church categorize HIV/AIDS positive people as beyond help because they believe they are waiting to die. As a result, they do not want to help them, claiming that they are wasting resources on already dead people. The church, as the body of Christ, must embrace, love, care for, and support HIV/AIDS positive people. In Christ, no one is turned away, and that attitude should be the attitude of the church. Bock writes,

> Jesus reaches out to those who are regarded as outsiders. He touches especially those whom others have often given up on. Similarly, our ministry needs to share the scope of audience that Jesus' ministry had... . The Samaritan knew God cared and that Jesus had a major role in that response... . He appreciated his restoration to life and expressed his appreciation to God and life through Jesus Christ. To understand the isolation that sin produces is to understand the freedom that salvation brings.[55]

The church should pursue the ministry that Christ began and complete it in its fullness to help, teach, preach, counsel, rebuke, build up, and be the light and salt of the world. This is the reason Christ coming and died—to reach out and save the lost, to bring those who are rejected by society into the kingdom of God.

Luke 10:27-30 NKJV: Good Samaritan

> The story of the Good Samaritan is a teaching lesson about the prejudice that people have towards others. According to biblical history, the Samaritans were considered by the Israelites as defiled and outcasts who had nothing to do with the kingdom of God. A certain lawyer wanted to trick Jesus about the inheritance of the kingdom of God. He quoted the Greatest Commandment, "You shall love the Lord your God with all your heart and with all your soul and with all your strength and with all mind and love your neighbor as you love yourself" (Matt 22:37 NKJV). He asked Jesus, "Who is my neighbor?" That was the breaking point. Jesus told a story about the Good

Samaritan who helped the wounded person, a Jew for that matter; he was left unconscious and the Good Samaritan helped him. The Good Samaritan took him to the inn and paid for his medical expenses. The same question is posed today to the church and the community to serve the needy and those who are stigmatized. Luke's form of quotation from Deuteronomy 6:5 is, indeed, interesting. A. R. C. Leaney writes,

According to the Halakah (the Jewish Law), this was for every fellow-countryman, not a non-Israelite. In the order of the human faculties, Luke followed a version of the Hebrew rather than the LXX; the clause, "and with your mind," is an addition, and the word for 'mind' is really an alternative translation of the Hebrew for "heart;" for no version in the OT knows of a form of the commandment in which four human faculties are mentioned.[56]

> In the natural sense, in Israel, Samaritans were believed to be helped rather than to help. A neighbor is anyone in needs help. Russell propounds,

Jesus' story of the Good Samaritan, recounted in Luke 10:25-37, is surely among the best known of New Testament passages... . The familiar story of the Good Samaritan has taken on new power as communities of people concerned about the AIDS crisis have shared their reflection on it with me.[57]

In a polarized society where racism, tribalism, and sexism are the order of the day and marginalization of one another happens daily, the story of the Good Samaritan teaches the church that it must not discriminate against anyone who needs assistance and to give a hand to neighbors regardless of race, beliefs, or other issues. The Good Samaritan saw the beaten and bruised man. He did not ask any questions, like why and how it happened, but he had compassion and cared for the victim. The Good Samaritan parable is meant to teach Christians and the church to make a difference in the hurting world.

> The strange behavior of the priest and Levite contrasts the attitude that the law required. The lawyer quoted what the law requires them to show in Deuteronomy 17:8.

Grace conquers sin and reconciliation brings mutual relationships. The lepers, and also HIV/AIDS-positive persons, need some help, love, and care. The AIDS crisis has curved the shape of ministry in the church today. Letty M. Russell states, "We are all living with AIDS, both as a worldwide health crisis and every community and church. Yet many churches still ignore this reality and practice a conspiracy of silence and rejection."[58] As AIDS began its merciless scourge, people seek a place to escape the mirage of misinformation, isolation, cruelty, and death. The church should be that place of that refuge. Russell writes,

> The spread of AIDS within our time is a crisis that may be changing our habitual way of looking at things. This crisis is an event of such magnitude that it is causing a paradigm shift, or a change of perspective. We see life through mental structures born of our experience and culture... . Living with AIDS presents to the dualistic perspective from which many Christians approach life, a perspective embedded in our New Testament tradition. AIDS is at present a terminal disease. Thus, it poses many questions about God and life in the face of seeming hopelessness. It presents

the church with a crisis of self- understanding through the discovery of the barriers our perspectives erect the ministry and caring.[59]

> The church continued isolating the Gentiles under the pressure from Jewish authorities to remain faithful to Jewish traditions. Russell continues, "According to Luke's description in Acts, the church was forced to follow where God was going, and to include those whom God was including in a mission to the Gentiles, in which the church was not sure it wanted."[60] The church is living through the call of God to holiness and it must present to, for, and with persons with AIDS. Those who are in Christ are called and empowered to the renewal of love in Christ. Russell writes,

The church is increasingly becoming the body of Christ, binding up the broken-hearted and healing the sick. The church has become the broken, tortured, bruised body of Christ restoring the world to him. The support and interaction offered by the churches can be an opportunity for positive spiritual experience in this time of crisis.[61]

Just as the members of the church with AIDS suffer discrimination in housing, employment, and medical care, the church suffers anti-AIDS discrimination in institutional forms. "Initiation of laws permitting pre-employment screening for AIDS antibodies were supported by 45 percent of those polled, although 51 percent favored laws protecting homosexuals from employment discrimination."[62] But the church has to stand up and support and care for the HIV/AIDS positive church members and condemn sin which is abomination to God.

> Some of the comments of the people infected by leprosy today include, "If we may be permitted to concisely state our cry, it is that even if we have leprosy we are still human beings."[63] Roberts A. Charlotte, Lewis E. Mary, and K. Manchester write,

To many of us, it is worse than the very disease is the prejudice that comes along with it. Many of us have stopped being called Francisco, Joe, Maria, and we are being called leprosy patient, 'lepers' and recently Hansenites…. I believe that our greatest challenge is to make sure that millions of people who have lost their identities will go back to be called by their own names.[64]

These sentiments come from people who have suffered isolation, stigmatization, and dehumanization because of their leprosy or HIV/AIDS status. The stigma that occurred in the Old and New Testaments still happens today to people with leprosy and HIV/AIDS.

Charlotte, Mary, and Manchester continue,

> A major step in eliminating the stigma associated with leprosy is by acknowledging that it affects millions of individuals with unique personalities and real names who were denied family, community and personal identity because they had a disease that was feared and misunderstood.[65]

Those who have leprosy today still suffer from isolation but not as much as in Old Testament times. HIV/AIDS patients are in similar situations in terms of discrimination. In counseling people with HIV/AIDS, "People are most likely to find personal meaning in a brief passage that they can repeat over and over again, and a passage of this nature can break up destructive mental and physical habit patterns and make a new perspective possible."[66] Counseling HIV/AIDS patients demands deep knowledge of the Scripture to relate to their situations. Capps elucidates,

> The Bible is the pastor's royal road to the deep levels of the personalities of his people, particularly to those who are deeply disturbed. Traditionally, the Bible has been used by ministers as a means of reassurance and comfort to people whom they visit and who come to them for counseling help.[67]

Biblically counseling HIV/AIDS patients requires the honest interpretation and application of the Scriptures. Capp continues, "The use of the Bible as an instrument of diagnosis, however, needs initial attention and extended study… . The integral relationship between the dynamic causes of the patients' illness and the use of that they make of Biblical material."[68] Concurring with Capps, one would reiterate the importance of application of the passage where it is appropriate in order to be honest with the Bible and the counselee.

The Church in Response to HIV/AIDS

The HIV/AIDS/Leprosy Challenge

The church has a vital role to combat HIV/AIDS disease by getting involved in counseling, praying, helping, and teaching the congregation about the dire situation caused by HIV/AIDS. Adams contends, "To pursue excellence in biblical counseling means to become *mahir* (proficient) in these tasks and thus to be *hikanos* (sufficient) so as to have *duunamis* (ability) necessary to carry them out."[69] To concur with Adams, biblical counseling, is the ability to apply Scripture in order to help the counselee in his/her challenging situation, in this case HIV/AIDS. To begin, sin is the cause of human suffering, which includes incurable diseases that have been unleashed on mankind because of disobedience. The concept in Genesis 3:17-19 NKJV points out that sin brought forth all forms of disorder and diseases that face each generation. HIV/AIDS is one of the incurable diseases that have befallen on mankind. "And there will be famines, pestilences, and earthquakes in various places" (Matt 24:7b NKJV). This portion of Scripture must not be taken out of context. It was Jesus who answered the question asked by his disciples about the signs and the time of his second coming. Jesus listed a number of them, of which was pestilences. Frumkin and Leonard write,

> HIV/AIDS is a chronic disease caused by the human immune deficiency virus (HIV). Acquired immune deficiency syndrome (AIDS) is a disease of the human immune system which is caused by the immune deficiency virus (HIV). The conditions progressively reduces the effectiveness of the immune system and leaves individuals prone to any types of diseases.[70]

By disobeying God, Adam brought misery to all humankind. Sin has taken a toll but there is hope in Christ in which God planned to redeem the human race through the promise of the coming of Jesus Christ. "For it is not possible that the blood of bulls and goats could take away sins" (Heb 10:4 NKJV). Christ had to come to give His life for the redemption of many. "For by one sacrifice he has made perfect forever those who are being made holy" (Heb 10:14 NIV). Jesus is the only answer and hope for those suffering from HIV.

There must be a meeting of man's problem and God's full solution in counseling.[71] HIV/AIDS has created a gap between healthy people and sick people, especially in Africa with regard to HIV/AIDS. The HIV/AIDS stigma plays an important role as those infected with the disease are reluctant to disclose their HIV/AIDS status. With leprosy in Israel, lepers also had brutal experiences as they were regarded as outcasts of society. The stigma of leprosy disease has some similarities with that of HIV/AIDS stigma. Leprosy has a unique progression in the skin:

> Leprosy is a chronic, mildly contagious granulomatous disease of tropical and subtropical regions, caused by the bacillus Mycobacterium leprae, characterized by ulcers of the skin, bone, and viscera and leading to loss of sensation, paralysis, gangrene, and deformation.[72]

Leprosy is also called Hansen's disease:

> Leprosy is a slowly progressing bacterial infection that affects the skin, peripheral nerves in the hands and feet, and mucous membranes of the nose, throat, and eyes. Destruction of the nerve endings causes the affected areas to lose sensation. Occasionally, because of the loss of feeling, the fingers and toes become mutilated and fall off, causing the deformities that are typically associated with the disease.[73]

Leprosy affects the body and also bears social stigma that breaks down relations in the family and society. The lepers are sometimes shunned by their families and society at large, leaving the victim socially isolated. Some accounts in the Bible can enhance the understanding of the sting of leprosy stigma.

> AIDS-related counseling includes home and hospital visitation, funerals, memorial services, and bereavement support. The church stands with the members and gives them moral and spiritual support when they are in need. Ministers, elders, and deacons should foster programs that administer support through volunteers and care givers. The church must set up programs for HIV/AIDS education to inform the church about the disease and how it should respond to members with the disease. Pamphlets and books, magazines, articles, and videos should be mobilized and distributed by the church to educate the members of the church on how to care and support the families, orphans, and the community affected. Sean Connolly states,

> A compassionate response is needed as well as political, financial, medical, psycho-social, and pastoral responses… . God calls us as the people of God to be ministers of compassion. God calls us to be prophetic where there is injustice and suffering…
> .
> God calls the church, the church that has AIDS to be a safe and supportive place.[74]

The church's focus should be to adopt positive programs in response to this epidemic.

The Leper Ostracized from the Society:
A Similar Stigma to HIV/AIDS

> The stigma associated with leprosy in Israel was a sad situation and the lepers were quarantined from the camp. France points out, "While the disease was probable not what is now technically called 'leprosy' the words 'leper' and 'leprosy' appropriately convey the social stigma attached to it in an age when precise medical diagnosis was not to be expected."[75] The HIV/AIDS stigma has

a negative social impact in the lives of those who are HIV/AIDS positive. France continues,

> With this condition it was different: as long as the condition persisted, the person had no place in society and had to contrive to exist away from other people's dwellings (Lev 13:45-46). No other disease carried this stigma, hence the horror with which the 'leper' was regarded.[76]

Leprosy carries the same stigma as of that of HIV/AIDS today. Frumkin and Leonard propound, AIDS has created enormous social and ethical dilemmas that defy simple solutions. The ethical dilemma of what constitutes the best care of the terminally ill person is a problem within medicine which has been heightened by the AIDS crisis.[77]

As a result, the stigma is widespread. "About 51 percent of American favored quarantine of those with AIDS, in a December 1985 *Los Angeles Times* Poll. The same percentage also favored a law making it a crime for a person with AIDS to have sex with another person." [78] Although the polls do not apply today, the AIDS stigma still exists. It mattered thirty years ago, and it still matters today.

> How did Jesus respond to the lepers' condition and stigma? France accounts Matthew,

> By recounting Jesus' response to the most feared and ostracized medical condition of his day, Matthew has laid an impressive foundation for this collection of stories which demonstrate both Jesus' unique healing power and his willingness to challenge the taboos of society in the interest of human compassion.[79]

The church, the bride of Christ, is obligated to respond to HIV/AIDS victims as Jesus responded to the lepers with social stigma. Witherington propounds,

> Jesus heals a man with a dreaded skin disease. Notice that Jesus reaches out and touches the man in order to heal him. Being unclean in a culture that focused on ritual impurity made one an outcast, literally an untouchable. Jesus believed that since the Dominion of God was breaking in, issues of ritual impurity were moot, and as such restrictions should be maintained. Jesus will advocate that only moral impurity defiles a person.[80]

The HIV/AIDS stigma is addressed here in the book of Matthew by Jesus Christ as he addressed the stigma of leprosy.

> Blomberg writes,

> Lepers were ostracized from society and lived in 'colonies.' They still exist in many parts of the world today, but the closest counterparts who most people are familiar may be AIDS victims. The leper in v. 2 displays a great audacity to mingle with such a crowd, in apparent defiance of Lev 13:46, but certainly treats Jesus with great

respect.[81] To reiterate Blomberg's assertion that the closest to the leper's counterparts are HIV/AIDS positive people affirms the similarities of their conditions in the public eye.

Christ expounded the biblical response to those who were stigmatized, isolated, and banished in society by healing and embracing them.

Lepers were treated the same in Israel in the Old Testament times and New Testament times. Hare summaries,

> In the Old Testament and later Jewish tradition, leprosy was often regarded as a punishment for sin (Num 12:10; II Kings 5:27).... At the theological level, the Gentile readers of the Gospel, excluded by Gentile uncleanness from Israel, would rejoice that the Messiah did not consider them unworthy but willed to cleanse the unclean and admit them to the kingdom.[82]

Just as the Israelites excluded the Gentiles and regarded the lepers as deserving punishment from God, the church in the early years of HIV/AIDS infections, condemned those with HIV/AIDS and regarded them as receiving God's punishment and judgment for their conduct. Moffatt writes,

> Each of these AIDS patients, living or dying, has brought the battle arena of AIDS out of the darkness into the light.... Because of the furor over AIDS as a loathsome plague, discrimination practices against AIDS patients have to be examined, and in some cases, changed for the better.[83]

> Caregivers should be trained within the church through medical experts on their work as caregivers. They are to demonstrate knowledge of the disease process, treatment, and the transmission factors of HIV. Caregivers have the capacity to identify issues facing HIV infected persons as well as ethical issues involved in AIDS care. It is fundamentally important that caregivers training in the church include care relationship dynamics in order to demonstrate the knowledge of the grief process and to connect the patients with the church for moral and spiritual support. A holistic plan of caring contributes to preventative medical practice as well as biblical counseling, pastoral care, and psycho-therapy. The church should also engage in referring HIV/AIDS positive members to clinics and hospitals to receive anti-viral drugs that decrease the fast progression of the disease. A relationship of trust and mutual respect should be fostered among patients, caregivers, and the church. Connolly writes,

> Sexual identity, recognition of one's drug addiction, family dynamics, social stigma and religious ideologies all play a major role in the psychological and social adjustment of the HIV affected person. The issue is best dealt with the HIV infected person and his/her medical personnel and/or professional counselor. Within the dynamics of the care relationship, empathy and support are major factors in helping someone with an education.[84]

In the story of the Good Samaritan, the one who was despised and an outcast is the one showing mercy and compassion to a Jewish stranger in need. The research reveals that those living with HIV/AIDS are the most active in support of others in the same situation. Religious stigma continues to be a psychological dilemma that HIV-infected persons must overcome and the church should stand by in support and care for them, in a holistic way. The model of the church is taken from Jesus who had unconditional love and embraced everyone and cared for all. HIV/AIDS has affected many countries in the world, however, some countries are still in the state of denial of its effect. Dube states,

> In a relatively short time, little more than two decades, HIV/AIDS has infected over 40 million people worldwide, claimed at least 22 million lives, orphaned 14 million children, brewed stigma and discrimination, and caused unimaginable human suffering.... It is not just a medical or biological issue. Rather, it is a social disease, which is very much dependent on poverty, violence, gender inequality, the abuse of human and children's rights, sexual discrimination, drug and sex trafficking, national corruption, international economic injustice, and globalization. It is a social injustices disease, which ironically promotes and perpetuates the social evils that create the environment in which it strive. It is a determinant and its magnitude have a far-reaching impact, affecting the economic, political, spiritual, social and cultural aspects of humanity and calling into question all the foundations of our relationships, including the vulnerability of occupying our own relationship.... This far-reaching impact means that we are all called to do the battle against the HIV/AIDS.[85]

> While it is true that social injustices, poverty, violence, gender inequality, and sexual discrimination are considered to be causes of the spread of HIV/AIDS, casual sex, stands as the main cause of spreading HIV/AIDS. Musa Wenkosi Dube writes,

> As reports of this immunodeficiency syndrome among homosexual individuals and intravenous drug users accumulated, it became apparent that the pattern of appearance of this disease was suggestive of a transmissible disease. The disease seemed to be spread through contact with semen or blood.[86]

The fundamental question posed in the context of HIV/AIDS is what the Bible says in the light of HIV/AIDS: "It is an invitation to biblical and theological scholars and religious leaders, in Africa and other continents, to own the struggle against HIV/AIDS."[87] The early interpretations of the Bible in light of HIV/AIDS were negative and promoted the stigma of those who were infected with the disease. Dube alludes to correct the early assumptions that HIV/AIDS was inflicted as a punishment to those who are infected:

It follows, therefore, that HIV/AIDS is not and cannot be a punishment sent by God, as some have alleged... . It is highly stigmatized and the infected are isolated, rejected or marginalized. They are sometimes considered sinners who deserve what they got. Many Christians interpret HIV/AIDS as a punishment from God.[88]

Some theologians relied on the passages and texts that associated sickness with God's punishment or judgment to those who are immoral and disobedient (Deut. 7:12-15 NKJV). It is fundamental to reflect on the context of the Bible about diseases such asHIV/AIDS and relate the biblical passages associated with the illness, disobedience, and punishment by God. The historical approach to assist and understand the context in which the passages were written is essential. A passage that sheds light in dealing with HIV/AIDS in the church is Mark 5:24b-43
NKJV. The two stories are about the bleeding woman and the dead young girl and how Jesus responded to the need. Christ is always the main character and he teaches how the church should response to immediate needs. Dube analyzes the situation:

> Here we are struck by doctors who cannot heal, patients who lose all their savings in the search for healing, the stigma that is attached to some illness, Jesus as a religious leader who is sensitive to the touch of a desperate woman and stops to listen, fathers who are actively involved in care, mourning communities who have lost their children, and the chilling reality of the death of young people. Reading the text in light of HIV/AIDS, we find similarities to our own critical situations and helpful models for hopeful and healing responses. [89]

Practical Response to HIV/AIDS through Biblical Counseling

In His sovereign grace, God has provided and equipped the church to response to the challenges the church may face. God calls men and women to serve others and not seek to be served or lauded above others. The ministry of encouraging is a vital arm of the church that helps those who are weak because of their situation and circumstances. Capps writes, "The Bible is to bring hope-giving comfort to counselees who are either going through typical crisis of life or are having to adjust to bereavement, divorce chronic illness, or physical handicaps."[90] Brooks explains, "Renounce the self as the dominant element in life. It is to replace the self with God-in-Christ as the object of affections. It is to place the divine will before the self-will."[91] God has given spiritual gifts to the church to edify, equip, encourage, love, and care for one another (Eph. 4:11 NKJV). The word "equip "in Greek, *katartismos*, means perfecting or conditioning. Spiritual gifts are used to fulfill the duties in the body of Christ and to build up the body of Christ. With HIV/AIDS wreaking havoc in the church and community, it is imperative to that people use their spiritual gifts to help others in need, especially people infected with HIV/AIDS. God gave spiritual gifts to the church to meet the needs of the believers and to edify the body of Christ. A spiritual gift is a special attribute given by the Holy Spirit to the church of Christ according to God's grace. Three key chapters discuss spiritual gifts: Romans 12, 1 Corinthians 12, and Ephesians 4
NKJV. The twenty-seven spiritual gifts are prophecy, service, exhortation, teaching, giving, mercy, wisdom, knowledge, faith, healing, miracles, discerning of spirits, tongues, apostle, interpreting the tongues, helps, administration, evangelist, pastors, celibacy, voluntary poverty, martyrdom, hospitality, missionary, intercession, leadership and exorcism. The following discussion on specific gifts is to anchor biblical counseling to HIV/AIDS positive patients who can be reached through the ministry of love, encouragement, giving, healing, helping, mercy, etc.

The Ministry of Loving Others

The Bible is the foundation to the counseling and response for the needs of society as a call for leadership to care for the people as Christ cared. In biblical counseling, WCC highlights some important points:

The church, by its very nature as the body of Christ, calls its members to become healing communities. Despite the extent and complexity of the problems raised by HIV/AIDS, the churches can make an effective healing witness towards those affected. The experience of love, acceptance and support within a community where God's love is made manifest can be a powerful healing force. This means that the church should not-as was often the case when AIDS was first recognized in the gay community—exclude, stigmatize and blame persons on the basis of behaviors which many local congregations and churches judge to be unacceptable. [92]

In critiquing WCC, one would argue that God and the church expect the transformation of behavior and godly life worthy of God's praise. The church should embrace, forgive, and love, but not condone any continued bad behavior and lifestyle that are contrary to the Bible. WCC writes, "When the church properly responds to people living with HIV/AIDS, both ministering to them and learning from their suffering, its relationship to them will indeed make a difference, and thus become growth-producing."[93]

The church is shaped by what Christ teaches and what he did, echoed by the disciples. It begins with the love that God manifested to the hurting world by sending Jesus Christ as a ransom for all. The three gospels (Matt 22:37, Mark 12:30, Luke 10:27, NKJV) allude to Jesus quoting Deuteronomy 6:5: "You shall love the Lord your God with all your heart, with all your soul, and with your entire mind." Jesus taught his disciples that this is the greatest and first commandment. Jesus also taught his disciples a second command, to "love your neighbor as yourself" (Matt 22:39; Mark 12:31 NKJV; Luke 10:27 NKJV). The second commandment teaches the church to take care of others, "My brother's keeper." To love a neighbor reveals the heart of God for believers. It directs the actions of believers to let their love for others flow from their love of God. The love of God in believers' lives must be lived and acted upon to fulfill the second Greatest Commandment. The church is the anchor of Christ to reach out to the needy. HIV/AIDS positive people deserve to be loved and cared for by the church and community. It is the high calling to serve Christ as He declared, "Just as the Son of Man did not come to be served, but to serve, and to give his life as a ransom for many" (Matt 20:28 NIV).

The Ministry of Encouraging Others

Paul identifies encouragement as one of the spiritual gifts in the church (Rom 12:8 NIV). "Encourage" in Greek, *parakaleo,* means to come to someone's aid or "calling someone to one's side."[94] The church should identify the members with the gift of encouragement to encourage and minister to HIV/AIDS positive people within the church and outside the church. Jesus and the Holy Spirit are Helpers (John 14:16; John 15:16 NKJV).
Jesus, as fully man and fully divine, encourages believers to persevere during trials and to overcome the temptations. The Holy Spirit, who lives in believers, encourages them to live righteous lives. "And he will be called Wonderful Counselor, Mighty God, Everlasting Father, Prince of Peace" (Isa 9:6 NIV). The Holy Spirit is the comforter and guides believers to all truth. "But I tell you the truth: It is for your good that I am going away. Unless I go away, the Counselor will not come to you; but if I go, I will send him to you," (John 16:7 NIV). HIV/AIDS positive people need to be advised on their actions and behavior. Christians are encouraged to live according to their beliefs and faith in Christ and their actions and behavior should be influenced by the Holy Spirit.

The Ministry of Giving

In the context of biblical counseling, HIV/AIDS patients cannot get adequate care and support without donation of funds, expertise, time, and human resources to prevent the spread of the disease. The HIV/AID epidemic needs financial, spiritual, moral, and social support from the church. The church should make a budget for assisting people with HIV/AIDS. Contribution to the needs of others is one of the gifts mentioned in the Bible. When giving to the church, one should give generously and sacrificially as to the Lord. This is voluntary giving of time, talent, and resources with liberality. It includes wisdom and knowledge that proves beneficial to those to whom one ministers. Paul encourages the church in Thessalonica about giving: "So, affectionately longing of you, we were well pleased to impart to you not only the gospel of God, but also our very lives because you had become very dear to us" (1 Thess. 2:8 NKJV). Paul refers to Moses' care to Israel as a nursing mother (Num. 11:12 NKJV). Paul talks about tenderness and intimacy with the church at Corinth, referring his love for them as that of the father to his children (2 Cor12:14-15 NKJV).

HIV/AIDS positive members of the church need love, care, and support from individuals, families, the community, and the church as a whole. Voluntary work therefore, is needed to discharge the gift. Volunteers who choose to work on certain 39 programs of the church are the means and ways of fostering fellowship. Luecke and Southard contend, "Participants in church programs are there because they feel something internally pushing them into action expressive of their life in Christ. The specific form of action they take on a given day is because of a pull exerted by others around them."[95]

There should be an internal push, pull, and passion for volunteers that are mostly suited for the program. Luecke and Southard explain, "To follow Christ includes heeding the call away from selfishness and toward selfless love of God and others. Christians should act according to God's call and the needs of their neighbors, not to satisfy their own needs."[96] The requirements are basic qualifications, commitment, effectiveness, efficiency, time, resources, and competency to get involved in serving others. Anthony and Estep write, "Synergy enables a team to accomplish more than the work of one individual or sum of individual contributions, becoming more than the sum of its parts."[97]

Working together as a team to give time and resources in order to help those in need is a noble Christian service. From the beginning of the church, people gave their time, resources, and talents freely to advance the kingdom of God. God has appointed leaders charged with equipping believers to do the work of service. Working with volunteers in the church involves four basic principles which include motivating, guiding, supporting, and supervising toward the volunteers' full potential in serving God through the church and the community.

The Ministry of Healing

Biblical counseling entails spiritual, psychological, and physical healing.

Hoffman propounds,

> Diseases such as HIV/AIDS profoundly affect the psychosocial, cultural, and political aspects of communities and countries. This worldwide pandemic has enormous implications for the health and psychosocial well-being of individuals, their family structures, and their community structures, for the delivery of psychosocial and medical services, and responses by government agencies.[98]

HIV/AIDS affects all aspects of life, which include emotional well-being, social support, and care for the victims. Biblical counseling draws the counselee into the Scripture to help him understand and see the light as God speaks through His Word. A compelling and powerful aspect of most spiritual traditions is the focus on healing rather curing.

Hofffman writes,

> Counseling interventions provides; ways to explore and address HIV-related concerns such as depression, and fears about the dying process, assistance with learning and maintaining self- and other protective practices, a means of emotional and social support.[99]

When the counselor attends to the counselee's problems, like having HIV/AIDS, he is dealing the whole being and the immediate family, including the community or church. The spiritual gift of healing in 1 Corinthians 12:9 NKJV indicates that through the work of the Holy Spirit Jesus can heal both spiritual and physical infirmities if he chooses to (Isa 53:4-5 NKJV). Grudem contends,

> Certainly it [the gift of healing] functions as a "sign" to authenticate the gospel message and show that the kingdom of God has come. Then also healing brings comfort and health to those who are ill, and thereby demonstrates God's attribute of mercy toward those in distress. Third, healing equips people for service, as physical impediments to ministry are removed. Fourth, healing provides opportunity for God to be glorified as people see physical evidence of his goodness, love, power, wisdom, and presence.[100]

> Jesus confronted an incurable disease, such as leprosy, with power and authority. He healed the ten lepers who were the outcasts of Israel. He did impossible things in the natural realms (Luke 17:12 NKV). Though Christ did not heal all the sick people in Israel, he can heal those he wants to heal. There is hope of total healing in Christ. However, while the church anticipates Christ to heal some individuals, caring for, supporting, and loving them are the

mandates? The church is to counsel, comfort, and to pray for those infected with HIV/AIDS as part of healing process. In Luke 10, Jesus sent seventy-two disciples and gave them the power and authority to proclaim and heal the sick. Matthew writes that Jesus healed the sick (8:16-17 NKJV). God can invade the natural realm whenever He wills to accomplish His purpose. He can heal HIV/AIDS according to His will and for His glory but if He chooses not to, the church, through members, must serve others to bring relief and hope.

The Ministry of Helping

In biblical counseling, the counselor applies biblical advice in light of the Scriptures, which involves taking the individual from the unknown to the known, which implies helping the counselee understand his situation, the need to confess and seek forgiveness. The ministry of help in the church occurs when the counselee receives spiritual and social support to overcome his predicament. Hoffman rightly states,

> Social support often acts as a buffer when people are in distress and positively affects psychosocial adjustment, perceptions of health status, and overall well-being.
> … Research has shown a relationship between HIV-infected persons' perceptions of social support and their reporting physical and psychological symptoms.101[101]

First Corinthians 12:28 mentions the gift of helping in the service of the church. The Greek word, *antilempsis*, refers to one person removing a burden from another and putting it on him/herself.[102] The church has people who are willing to alleviate burdens on some people and carry the burden for the sake of the service for the glory of God. HIV/AIDS patients who are home-bound need such service. Caregivers help those who are homebound and not able to fend for themselves because of AIDS. They are to be fed, bathed, and given medication in their homes. Those who have the gift of assisting others are willing to do anything in order to help those who are in need. "The one gifted with helps is marked with a generous spirit and utilizes his gift with great joy, usually and even preferably, in unnoticed ways, or behind the scenes."[103] They recognize needs and are quick to respond to those needs with support. "It is more blessed to give than to receive," (Acts 20:35 NKJV). Paul encouraged Christians to "help those who are weak in faith" (Romans 15:1 NKJV).

The Ministry of Mercy

Biblical counseling is showing the love and mercy of God from the Bible to a HIV/AIDS patient who may have lost hope in God. God is a merciful has people at heart. With that powerful meaning of love, God must be portrayed in the church, the love from body of Christ. Ronald Nicolson writes, "Why indeed should God be mindful of a human race that with AIDS has found yet another way to destroy itself?"[104] Nevertheless, God has extended His mercy to all people, even those who are the victims of HIV/AIDS. The church through biblical counseling teaches through the church God's mercy. The gift of mercy is one of the gifts cherished by the church, as mentioned in Romans 12:8. The gift is to administer help and kindness to those in need. In the New Testament, mercy is used to describe the act of giving to poverty stricken individuals. Those with HIV/AIDS use all their resources in search of medications, like antiviral drugs, to slow the progression of HIV. Those endowed with the gift of mercy generously give and assist those in need. Showing mercy is not only done financially but through other forms of help. Isaiah 1:17 NKJV, commands believers to defend widows and care for them. There are about three million HIV/AIDS children in Zimbabwe and widows are left in desperate need of help. Moses declared in Deuteronomy 10:17 NKJV that God will defend the fatherless. The church has a huge ministry to show mercy and assist orphans and widows. God declared Himself the father to the fatherless (Psalms 68:5 NKJV).

HIV/AIDS and Leprosy Compared

In recent years, AIDS has been paralleled as the leprosy of our time. Nicolson authenticates this statement: "The analogy between AIDS and leprosy has been noticed by a number of people.... . Leprosy in the Bible was a disease for which there was then no cure, though sometimes people could spontaneously recover."[105] The lepers could not mix with society because they were regarded as unclean. As result, they were banished from the camp until certified by the priests as no longer a danger to society. In the same way, in the early discovery of HIV/AIDS, there was isolation of those diagnosed with

HIV/AIDS. Nicolson writes,

In the South Africa prison system, for example, persons with HIV/AIDS are kept in cells apart from other prisoners for fear of that they might pass on the infection—but also for their own protection, since if other prisoners knew they were HIV positive their lives would be in dangers.106[106]

The stigma of both leprosy and HIV/AIDS strike the similarities. Robin Gill propounds,

"In the context of HIV/AIDS, the most powerful obstacle to effective prevention, treatment and care is proving to be the stigmatization of people living with HIV/AIDS."[107] Compared to leprosy, HIV/AIDS victims are isolated into their own social structure. While the lepers were isolated physically and socially in Israel, HIV/AIDS positive people are isolated socially, especially in the first discovery of HIV/AIDS. Nicolson propounds,

Although AIDS and HIV were quite unknown in the Bible times, and although our context is so different, we do find in all sorts of ways that reflection on the Bible helps us see AIDS and people with AIDS in a new and different way from before.

> The dialogue between text and present context bring new light to both the text and the situation in which we find ourselves.[108]

The consequence of stigmatization is discrimination. In the process, stereotypes are damaging and as a result, injustice and discrimination occur. Sometimes Christians present God as a monster who inflicts people with HIV/AIDS as punishment or judgment for sin. Sometimes churches misinterpret Scripture to suit their own style of worship and in the process stigmatize people living with HIV/AIDS. Gill points out,

> It is not possible to find, in the Bible, an exact parallel to stigmatization of those with HIV/AIDS: and yet within the biblical tradition there are many examples that point to the way in which the stigmatized of the day were treated. We need to learn from the manner in which Jesus related to and responded to the stigmatized, for example, to the lepers, Samaritans, a menstruating woman, and those with physical and emotional disabilities.[109]

Jesus loved those who were stigmatized by society. He invited them, went to their homes, ate with them, touched them and they touched Him (Mark 6:56 NKJV). The church should do likewise. If Jesus embraced the stigmatized, the church should also open the arms to welcome, teach, love, and care for them. God's love and justice is portrayed throughout the Bible. The incarnation of Christ ushers new hope and restoration through His death and resurrection. Gill writes,

> It is wrong to interpret HIV/AIDS (or other human catastrophes) as God's punishment for sin. This interpretation is damaging, because the judgmental attitudes that result are highly undermining to the Church's efforts at care and prevention.[110]

Job was stigmatized by his friends, his community, and by his wife. The result of stigmatization is isolation, denial, and fear to be open with one's HIV/AIDS status and then avoid any kind of help. The church usually deals with the symptoms and does not want to deal with the causes of the disease. As the church engages in dialogue with the community about HIV/AIDS, it is fundamentally important for the church to rediscover its mandate and become a prophetic voice. Frumkin and Leonard write,

> AIDS has created enormous social and ethical dilemmas that defy simple solutions. The financial burden that AIDS has placed on the health care system has made funding quality patient care even more difficult than before... . AIDS is a long prolonged illness that involves great suffering for patients, friends, and families.[111]

Embracing HIV/AIDS Positive People in the Church

The church is the community of believers who serve Christ through serving others in the church and outside the church. When some members of the church have HIV/AIDS, the church embraces and welcomes them. Frumkin and Leonard expound,

> Throughout the Christian Bible, Jesus is portrayed as caring for and listening to people by entering into relationships with them. Entering into a care relationship can include hospital/nursing home visitation, being a care giver to someone who is ill ... making dinner for a family.... . Pastoral care relationships are built much like friends.[112]

Pastoral care relationships include caring, empathy, trust, mutual respect, and love. The church is the bride of Christ and therefore, it represents Christ on earth in caring for those in need. It must embrace rather than reject. It must love instead of hate. It must care instead of neglect. It must give instead of get. It must forgive instead of making grudge. These are the characteristics of the church that represents Christ. During the process of counseling, some fundamental principles need to be carried out. Eye contact with the client is very important. Listening and response techniques are very important also in caring for HIV/AIDS positive people. Listening to what is being communicated and probing questions can assure the patient that the other is listening and that he/she is concerned about the condition of the person. Biblical counseling includes adopting some options to care for HIV/AIDS positive people which must come from medical professions, the community, and the church. It is a combined effort to care for those suffering from the disease. Some physicians are reluctant to treat patients with the disease, citing high risks. However, with education concerning the disease, reluctance is slowly going away. The medical provides the medicine for patients. The religious gives spiritual support and counseling. The society and communities give moral support. Everyone should be involved and the church is the salt of the world to embrace, love, and care for those with HIV/AIDS.

The cost to care for patients is huge and consists of human resources, financial resources, and moral support. People with HIV/AIDS are usually depressed and in some cases they have suicidal ideation. Meeting and counseling is important. Public attitudes about HIV/AIDS play crucial roles in shaping the nation's response to those who are infected. Tolerance of people with HIV/AIDS in public places, homes, and institutions can enhance confidence and freedom of association with other people thus fostering relationships.

The church does not have an excuse. It has to respond to the needs of the people in the community and within itself. Hall and others contend,

Today, as many as 46 million people are infected with the AIDS virus. If Jesus, in the parable of the Good Samaritan, did not distinguish whether he was the victim because of sinful behavior or innocent victim, should we? We are bound by Scripture to respond to all those beaten and left by this devastating virus. [113]

Care and support of orphans and vulnerable children are important in preventing the cycles of disease and poverty. Institutional care has proven to be undesirable because it detaches children from communities and social connections. It is also very expensive to run these institutions. Community-based care is the best strategy for caring for orphans. The church demonstrates Christ's love, care, and support whenever it engages in the lives of those who HIV/AIDS positive.

In other countries, the response is tremendous toward curbing the spread of HIV/AIDS. In Zimbabwe, for example, the government has initiated some counseling programs. UNICEF confirms,

> In 2010, the government launched the HIV testing and counseling campaign (HCT), part of a process of meeting the targets set out in the National Strategic Plan (NSP). Each person receiving counseling and testing was to receive 100 condoms, with the campaign involving a host of other prevention initiatives such as information, education and mass mobilization.[114]

The church and the government of Zimbabwe have cooperated in the effort to prevent the spread of HIV/AIDS, although their approaches are different. In recent years, there have been some relative decline in HIV/AIDS infections. The use of condoms and sexual behavioral change has resulted in the decline in HIV infections in Zimbabwe. The National AIDS Council explains,

> However, regarding HIV and AIDS, the country is currently seeing some progress and improvements; Zimbabwe is one of the few countries where incidence has declined by more than 25 percent between 2001 and 2009. This is partially due to efforts among the population to prevent the spread of HIV, some of which have been remarkable in the context of such immense challenges.[115]

By 2009, about one million children living in Zimbabwe had been orphaned as a result of parents dying from AIDS. The National AIDS Council continues,

> Efforts to prevent the spread of HIV in Zimbabwe have been spearheaded by the National AIDS Council, non-governmental, religious and academic organizations. Prevention schemes have been significantly expanded since the turn of the millennium, but remain critically under-funded. Although mortality rates have played a large part in reducing the number of people living with HIV among the population of Zimbabwe, it is believed prevention programs aimed at behavior change and the prevention of mother to child transmission have also been instrumental in bringing about a decline in HIV prevalence.[116]

Embracing HIV/AIDS positive people not only includes caring for and meeting needs but also HIV/AIDS education:

> Children in Zimbabwe are currently taught about HIV and AIDS in schools. In 2006, the Ministry of Education, Sport and Culture, and UNICEF initiated an in-service training scheme of primary and secondary school teachers in HIV and AIDS life-skills and counseling. By the end of 2007 around 2753 primary and secondary schools had been reached by the scheme.[117]

The government emphasized the importance of voluntary counseling and testing for HIV (VCT) in its National AIDS Policy in 1999.[118] Anti-retroviral drugs are administered to HIV/AIDS positive people to slow the progression of the disease. Despite a high level of awareness, HIV and AIDS remain highly stigmatized in Zimbabwe. People living with HIV are often perceived as bad people with bad behavior, hence the rise of discrimination. Many people are afraid to be tested for HIV/AIDS, having fear of being socially alienated and discrimination. Those who do know about their HIV/AIDS status rarely let anyone know even their closest friends, spouse, children, or relatives. The church then comes in to counsel and direct them to Christ. When the world rejects, the church embraces, giving spiritual, moral, and social support.

Conclusion

The biblical and theological foundation for counseling those with HIV/AIDS and leprosy have similar stigma, hence, creating an opportunity for the church to serve. Scientists speculate that AIDS first appeared in America among homosexuals. There is no known source as to when and how HIV/AIDS originated and there is still no cure for it. Leprosy was a disease characterized by stigma, and HIV/AIDS also has strong stigma.

The Bible is read in search of answers to all of life's questions. The interpretations of the Bible in light of HIV/AIDS were negative and promoted the stigma of those infected with the disease. As Christ has taught his church to love, care for, and support those who are suffering, it imperative for the church to see to it that no one left out. The church should embrace HIV/AIDS positive patients as Christ taught about the Good Samaritan and other situations in the Bible to show God's mercy and compassion. HIV/AIDS positive people deserve to be loved and cared for by the church and the community. The church must set up programs to educate church members about HIV/AIDS and how they should respond to members infected with the disease. Caregivers have the capacity to identify issues facing HIV infected persons as well as ethical issues involved in AIDS care. Pastoral care relationships include caring, empathy, trust, mutual respect, and love. The church is the bride of Christ and therefore, it must embrace rather than reject everyone.

CHAPTER 3

SOCIAL RESPONSE TO HIV/AIDS THROUGH BIBLICAL COUNSELING

The social response to HIV/AIDS through biblical counseling is a response to people with HIV/AIDS in the light of Scripture and social interventions. Mary Ann Hoffman writes,

> In this way, diseases such as HIV profoundly affect the psychosocial, cultural, and political aspects of communities and countries. Moreover, the meaning attached to a particular disease, such as HIV, affects how those who are afflicted perceive and are perceived by other.[119]

When a person finds out that he/she has HIV/AIDS, many think their world has come to an end. Because of this, some may attempt to end their lives by committing suicide. There are many reasons why people want to end their lives after learning that they are HIV/AIDS positive, but the main reason has to do with the stigma. The value of knowing one's HIV/AIDS status, examining available interventions to combat HIV/AIDS, and counseling those who have stress and depression because of HIV/AIDS will be discussed in this chapter. This chapter also expounds on counseling HIV/AIDS positive church members. The chapter further discusses the counseling of children facing death, the challenges of women with HIV/AIDS, and how to counsel church members who have suicidal thoughts because of HIV/AIDS.

Counseling HIV/AIDS Church Members to Cope with Stress and Depression

When HIV/AIDS comes into a family, each member of the family is affected and traumatized emotionally, spiritually, and physically. If the family is affected by the disease, the church is also affected. Sheri Johnson and Adele Hayes write,

> Because of its prevalence, depression has been described as the common cold of mental illness. To receive a diagnosis of major depression, an individual must experience the following symptoms for a period of 2 weeks or more: sad mood or loss of pleasure, with at least four other symptoms such as sleep disturbance, appetite or weight changes, psychomotor agitation, or retardation, fatigue, feelings of worthlessness or guilt, diminished ability to think or concentrate, and recurrent thoughts of death or suicide.[120]

To deal with depression, a counselor should know a number of factors, including an assessment of the period of the disease one has discovered he/she has, family ties and relationships, the individual's financial resources and assets, faith and belief in God, and how one views his/her sickness.

Depression as a Social Issue

> The origin of depression varies from individual to individual and society to society. In reference to HIV/AIDS, when someone has been diagnosed with the disease, they encounter a number of challenges which acerbate depression. The HIV/AIDS patient thinks deeply as to how he/she contracted the disease, why it happened to him/her, and he/she wants to find a solution for it. When they spend much time thinking about how and why they contracted the disease, they fall into depression. Janice Wood Wetzel explains,

Our knowledge of depression dates back to 1033 B.C. in the Old Testament where King Saul in the book of 1 Samuel 16:14-23 recounts recurrent symptoms depression and suicide... . For the first time, the mental disorders were attributed to brain pathology which in turn was said to affect thought and action.[121]

HIV/AIDS victims suffer from depression because they are sad that sooner or later they will die. They ponder death, day and night, reflecting on their past experiences with regret and thinking of the future without their children, spouses, and family members. These thoughts flash through their minds all the time and affect their emotions, thus creating depression. Some can conceal depression consciously while others hide behind a mask of denial. Wetzel continues,

> In all cases, gentle probing will reveal a dysphonic mood state, replete with anxiety, guilt, and resentment... . Difficulty with thinking processes is characteristic of almost all depressed people. Problems with concentration and decision making are a direct result. Negative rumination about the world, the self, and the future has been casually linked to depression as well, often encouraged recurrent suicidal thoughts.[122]

Social withdrawal is a common behavior associated with depressed people who might have lost interest in social activity and relationships of all kinds. For some, their motor responses are grossly affected while others are easily agitated, hostile, or irritated. As a result, physical function is also affected. Wetzel outlines diagnostic signs and symptoms of depression:

> Affective feeling state of sadness, dejected, fearfulness, anxiety, inadequacy, anger, guilt, confusion, tiredness, hopelessness, irritability. Cognitive thoughts process; negative view of the world, irrational beliefs, recurrent thoughts of death, self-reproach, low self-esteem, denial, slow thinking, disinterest in activities (people, pleasure), confused thoughts, poor concentration, agitation. Behavioral activity; dependence, submissiveness, poor communication skills, controlled by others, crying, withdrawal, inactivity, careless appearance, slowed motor responses. Physical functioning; low energy, weakness, fatigue sleep disturbance, weight loss, fatigue, appetite disturbance, indigestion, constipation diarrhea, nausea, muscle aches and headaches, tension, sex-drive disturbance.[123]

The Symptoms of Depression

Depression symptoms are synonymous with HIV/AIDS. The pastor or counselor must be able to know the symptoms in order to counsel with informed observation and knowledge of what he/she is dealing with. As much as the member of the church may not disclose his/her HIV/AIDS status, the counselor must be able to probe with wisdom. Hoffman asserts,

> Emotional distress is common when people learn that they have HIV disease... . Other occurrences related to HIV disease, such as experiencing stigmatization or rejection or losing social support, can also create a sense of emotional disequilibrium. It may not even be clear what has triggered this intense and powerful awareness. Thus, one of the hallmarks of HIV disease is this experience of disequilibrium.[124]

The Effects of Depression on HIV/AIDS Patients

Depression affects the mind, emotions, and soul. The psyche of a human being can be affected by circumstances and situations, hence stress and depression are the result of such psychological disorder. Nerve cells communicate to each other through electrical signals and brain chemicals. The following diagrams show the normal nerve cell communication in thebrain. The brain functions normal. R. Ingalla and N. Oliver explain,

This brain chemical then docks onto receptors of a second nerve cell. If enough chemical attaches on to the receptors, the second nerve cell is activated if it wasn't removed, the chemical would keep docking onto the receptors and nerve communication would be a constant nonsensical 'chatter' if a nerve cell is unhealthy (i.e. not working well), it generally has less receptors on its surface this makes it difficult for chemicals to attach and activate the nerve cell and keep the chain reaction going. A nerve cell that isn't activated on a regular basis becomes more and more unhealthy and can eventually delete unhealthy nerve cells in the brain are unlikely to have a major impact on overall brain function, but if many nerve cells in one brain area aren't working properly, effects can become very bad this is what happens in depression; the nerve cells in certain areas of the brain are unhealthy and not working properly.[125]

Figure 2 illustrates how depression occurs on the individual who has become chemically unbalanced. Figure 1 illustrates normal nerve cells 1 to nerve cell 2.[126]

Counseling the individual can be therapeutic, but if the depression is beyond reach, it may require medication. Figures 2 shows the process and impact if depression has not been addressed.[127] It is important to understand the process and what the member of the church goes through when being counseled, because depression is the number one culprit in shortening the life of HIV/AIDS positive patients and a cause of death. The skills of the counselor need to be of that of a professional counselor in order to get the best result for the counselee and the family members who anticipate full recovery and a better future. In the figure, the brain should receive enough oxygen and fuel needed for the brain to function well. R. Ingall and N. Oliver explain, "Diagram 2 shows the attempted activation of an unhealthy nerve cell without anti-depressant medication; diagram 3 shows the same, but with anti-depressant medication."[128]

The attempted activation with antidepressant medication does not necessarily bring normality or stability. Through biblical counseling, the patient can come in grips with reality and recover from depression as the counselor helps the counselee to heal.

Redirecting the Counselee to Christ:
Counseling Depression

In biblical counseling, the Scriptures point the HIV/AIDS positive church member to Christ when he/she is facing death. "The thief on the cross looked to Jesus and asked, 'Jesus, remember me when you come into your kingdom.' Jesus answered, him, "Today you be with me in paradise" (Luke 23:42-43 NIV). When someone has lost hope in life, the counselor must refer or redirect the counselee to Christ because he is the bread of life, and the living water: "I am a good shepherd; I know my sheep and my sheep know me," (John 10:14-15 NIV). Christ is the resurrection and life. "I am the resurrection and the life. The one who believes in me will live, even though they die" (John 11:25 NIV).

How does one counsel those who are depressed because of HIV/AIDS? The first tool to be used is the Bible, the Word of God. Teaching members to cast their burdens on Christ is the first instruction to be shared with the depressed (Matt 11:28 NKJV). Job's three friends gave him bad counsel, accusing him of sinning against God (Job 2:11-13 NKJV). The first friend, Eliphaz, accused Job of sinning against God and of folly and said that therefore he was chastised by God; Job refuted the notion. The second friend, Bildad, accused Job of sinning and told him that he needed to repent because the wicked are punished; Job refused to listen to the accusation and pleaded with God instead. The third friend, Zophar, also urged Job to repent of his sins against God because he was wicked; Job answered his critics and maintained his integrity. His wife also asked him to curse God and die but Job refused and did not sin against God. Job demonstrates the love of God, perseverance, endurance, faith in God, and trusting the Lord in every circumstance. The counselor can refer the counselee to Job as an example of not giving up faith in God.

> In order to assist HIV/AIDS positive people, certain counseling skills are required. Demitri Papolos and Janice Papolos state,

> In the most fundamental sense of the word, psychotherapy is a dialogue between two people where the patient has the respectful attention of a professional trained to elicit information. The professional, through clarification and interpretation, helps the person see things about him or herself in a realistic light-one not by a lingering sense of worthlessness or victimization... . Psychotherapy can strengthen the capacity to cope, help the person to understand and come to terms with the vulnerability, and develop an adaptive way of coping with interpersonal problems that emerge or are magnified as a result of the illness. [129]

In biblical counseling, the approach is Bible-oriented. Family members can support the patient if they are given information, for family involvement makes a critical difference in the life of an HIV/AIDS positive person. In counseling HIV/AIDS positive church members, it is imperative to actively involve family members. The counselor guides and encourages the sick person to cope with the disease and to deal with anxiety, emotions, and frustration. Papolos and Papolos write,

There are stages of recognition, adjustment, and adaptation to illness and each family travels through the stages in its own time and in its own fashion. Many factors influence the family's initial response to the onset of the illness: some members need to protect with the cloak of denial; almost all invent theories or take responsibility in an attempt to explain the changes in behavior. Each family is actually a caretaking system that over time has established rules, expectations, and basic assumption about caring for each other.[130]

> There is a cultural tendency, especially in Zimbabwe, to attempt to shield children from the unpleasant realities of life and of the illness at home. However, children are very sensitive and can imagine fast and terrible things about what would happen if their father or mother dies. Children become confused and anxious about their future. If their emotions explode, they are filled with fear, anxiety, uncertainty, and confusion.

There is a need for gradual explanation from one parent about the challenges and the predicament they would face. Children who participate and are involved in their parents' health challenges, happiness, and sorrows usually develop strength and a sense of belonging and worthiness when confronted with death. They are more able to cope with the death of loved ones than those who are left in the dark.

The church becomes the larger family to console, comfort, guide, counsel, pray for, encourage, empower, and support those members with HIV/AIDS. The children, orphans, widows, and widowers should find refuge in the church. The pastor or counselor should prepare those who are dying to put their hope in Christ as they share the everlasting love and grace of Christ Jesus.

Sexual Behavioral Change of HIV/AIDS Positive Members

When someone changes his/her sexual lifestyle and becomes responsible about his/her sexual behavior, there is imminent change for the better. Counseling HIV/AIDS using Scriptures helps the counselee to see his/her problem in the light of the Bible. Schepp contends, "Good counseling requires listening, empathy, and rapport building before most treatment approaches are effective."[131] It took many years for people to accept HIV/AIDS counseling because they were afraid of stigmatization. It has been discovered that if one partner is infected with the virus, condoms can prevent further infections to another partner who is not HIV positive. If the couple is married, the use of condoms to prevent further infection is recommended. If couples do not use condoms, infection increases and immunity is decreased, thus, leaving the couple prone to other diseases that may eventually kill them earlier than expected. Sometimes good information will not be sufficient to resolve a sexuality-related concern because the clients may be still in a denial stage. However, the counselor should probe and help the patient to reach a level to accept his/her HIV/AIDS status and condition and then accept counseling and advice.

Change of Heart, Attitude, and Action to Curb HIV/AIDS

As HIV/AIDS spreads rapidly, biblical counselors can foster change of heart and attitude toward curbing the disease by referring patients to Christ to seek forgiveness and be transformed by the Holy Spirit. Unprotected sex is the highest rate in which HIV/AIDS is transmitted, but there are other ways in which it is transmitted, such as by using the same needles as infected persons, through blood transfusion, through body fluids such as semen, breast feeding (infant-mother transmission), and by using the same razor blade as an infected person. When one discovers that he/she has HIV/AIDS, there is need for sexual behavioral change. The church teaches a change of heart and lifestyle for believers. If a member of the church is not faithful to his wife or her husband, the church must disciple, pray, and counsel to change lifestyle and to trust God. To youth, the church teaches sexual abstinence before marriage and to flee youthful lusts, as the Bible teaches. If there is a change of sexual behavior, change of heart by spiritual transformation, and concerted efforts to curb the new HIV/AIDS infection, there is hope that the disease will decrease and a new generation which is free from HIV/AIDS will be the remnant. For those who are HIV/AIDS positive, the church teaches protected sex, faithfulness within marriage, living holy lives, and presenting their bodies as a living sacrifice, all for the glory of God.

The counselor needs to be knowledgeable to reassure the clients that HIV/AIDS is not contracted by shaking hands or sharing the same utensils with the patient. Church members with HIV/AIDS need support and advice on sexual decision making, because patients react with panic, fear, grief, anger, and guilt about their future. The counselor should be bold in confronting these issues. When a responsive client accepts the advice about his/her sexual behavior, it is a therapy on its own. A person can be taught a thousand lessons, but if he/she does not internalize and put the lessons into practice, he/she will remain the same. Conviction and acceptance of one's condition and situation can make a great change. Brenda Almond writes,

> The spread of HIV is in essence through private consensual contact. Only through an understanding, by both counselor and individual, of the nature of such contacts, and relevant advice on behavioral change do we have any chance of influencing the spread of HIV. A person's ability to effect such behavioral change will be affected by comprehension and motivation. Tools to assist in the achievement of behavioral change will necessarily be diverse, according to individual personal and context attributes.[132]

Almond suggests that every person has the ability to change his/her behavior to protect himself/herself and also others through HIV/AIDS prevention. This change occurs more so, through the help of the Holy Spirit and through biblical counseling.

HIV/AIDS voluntary testing is one of the best ways to foster prevention.

HIV/AIDS testing gives individuals information about their HIV/AIDS status; hence they will make an informed decision about sexual behavior. Almond expounds,

> As experience increases and as social attitudes change, take-up of HIV testing is increasingly well-informed and secured. However, it must remain a matter for the individual to balance the pros and cons and to adopt behavioral change regardless of the decision taken.[133]

Sexual behavioral change by HIV/AIDS positive church members and the general populace can make a difference in the family, church, and in the community. However, sexual behavior must change as soon as one discovers he/she has HIV/AIDS. Almond points it out,

> Generic counseling involves helping people to live with uncertainty. The language of the generics is the language of 'might' and 'may." ... Living with uncertainty, and making decision in the face of uncertainty, presents particular problems for the individual concerned.[134]

HIV/AIDS prevention is very important when one plans to have a family. When couples get married and decide to have children, they should know their HIV/AIDS status. With the prevalence of HIV/AIDS, it is important to make those decisions wisely. Decisions vary from family to family and from individual to individual. For those who are still young and want to have children, preventing any HIV/AIDS infection is vital during pregnancy. It is possible through medical prevention, making sure that the fetus is not infected. The biblical counselor can help couples to make those decisions.

Community of Believers

In biblical counseling, when the patient has been counseled, he/she goes back to the community where he/she belongs and is assimilated into that culture. In the body of Christ, the church members belong together and are each other's "brother's keepers." The community of believers cares for and supports one another. When a member has been diagnosed with HIV/AIDS, he/she should be shown to live a positive life. "Just as a body, has many parts, but all its parts form one body, so is it with Christ" (1 Cor 12:12 NIV). The church members should care for and support one another. People experience joy when they are surrounded by loved ones, but fear and anxiety creep in when the bond is ruptured. A human being is a physical being, a social being, and a spiritual being. The community that surrounds him/her can give him/her a sense of belonging, and security is important. Leslie Greenberg states,

> Human beings need others to feel secure and happy. Healthy adult attachment and intimacy involve emotional availability and responsiveness, security and warmth. The need for other people becomes unhealthy only when a person cannot tolerate separation and flies into rage or becomes depressed at loss, separation, or distance.[135]

When counseling HIV/AIDS positive members in the church, emotions are the windows of what the person is going through. A counselor must observe emotions when counseling HIV/AIDS positive people to know whether they have been hurt or are avoiding actions to engage in sexual behavioral change. Greenberg states, "Once hurt, many people vow never again to let themselves be vulnerable protective stance that is driven by a fear of intimacy. People fear emotional intimacy mainly because they fear being hurt again."[136]

Repentance and Forgiveness

> In biblical counseling, counseling people with HIV/AIDS means fostering spiritual restoration and soul healing. Jesus is presented as the Savior, mediator, Lord of all and the Way, the Truth and the Life (John 14:6 NKJV). The Holy Spirit is presented as the one who indwells in us and cleanses us from all unrighteousness. He leads to all truth.

Soul healing is a spiritual phenomenon, initiated by God through the Holy Spirit. Men cannot induce soul healing. Beaver writes,

> Indeed, through helping clients to accept death we may facilitate the desired wholeness or balance. However, in our own role as counselors/therapists, we are not

the healers. Rather, we become conduits for healing in a process that is shared with the clients. As part of the process, we invite the clients to become curators of their own souls and to understand the ability they have to influence their own healing.[137]

HIV/AIDS position persons have to decide to change their sexual behaviors. The repercussions are disastrous to family members, the church, and the community if they refuse to change their sexual behaviors.

Counseling Children with HIV/AIDS

It was in 2003 when I was officiating the wedding of the niece of now President of Zimbabwe, Emmerson Mnangagwe when he said that the government's hope is in the church because of its teachings of biblical and moral values. He said that the government was overwhelmed by the HIV/AIDS epidemic. Christians have been infected just as other people in the country, but it was interesting to hear a government official acknowledge that the church is the only hope in times of the HIV/AIDS crisis. The goal of Zimbabwe is to be HIV/AIDS free by year 2030. Will that goal be reached? The government of Zimbabwe has indeed introduced programs, information, and education to teach its people about prevention through interventions that have recorded a decline of HIV infection by 15.6 percent from 2003 to 2007. The government of Zimbabwe, through the Ministry of Health and Child Welfare, has joined together with the church and non-governmental organizations in an effort to curb the epidemic. The most affected age group with HIV/AIDS infections are children because they are vulnerable, defenseless, and most are in poverty and are voiceless. In 2009, there were more than one million orphans as a result of AIDS in Zimbabwe.[138]

HIV/AIDS Infection and Children

Children have been victims of HIV/AIDS, and they get the virus from their mothers before birth or after birth through breast feeding. Helen Land writes,

> By far the vast majority of infected children (nearly 85%) acquire the virus from their mother before or at birth ... Such transmission is variously called vertical, intrauterine, transplacental, prenatal, and congenital, reflecting uncertainty about how and when transmission from mother to child occurs."[139]

Mother to child transmission was high until in 1999, when the mother-to-child-transmission (MTCT) drug program was launched. Antiretroviral drugs (ARVs) have also helped the mortality rate.[140] But still, children born into families with one parent or both having HIV/AIDS disease face hunger, abuse, neglect, sickness, and death every day. Traditionally, it is a taboo in Zimbabwe to discuss death with the children. If a parent, uncle, cousin, grandmother, or grandfather dies, children are informed that those who have died went to a far country and would take a long time to come back.

However, it has been discovered that it is unfair not to tell children about the death of their parents and themselves. Papadatou and Papadatos state,

> Death is a universal and inevitable process that must be faced by people of all ages. Children who are able to participate with their families, after the death of someone they love, will be better equipped to understand and manage the emotions of their grief.[141]

Counselors have to understand that good mental health is not the denial of tragedy, but is confronting the pain of separation associated with death, even to children. Children should also be taught the consequences of HIV/AIDS, although usually parents who are HIV/AIDS positive do not like to disclose their status to their children. When HIV/AIDS status is disclosed to their children by the parent or parents before they die, it is a good opportunity to tell them about the dangers of contracting HIV/AIDS.

> A counselor or the pastor of a church must have a good rapport between the parents of the children of every family and the children themselves. There must also be a conversation about the value of children in a home and their contributions, adolescent challenges and how to overcome them, choosing a life partner, marriage, divorce, and death. These conversations help ease the tension when reality comes into effect. Children need to be prepared for bad times and good times in life. Grief and emotions are experienced by every human being and they are normal. Both adults and children experience grief and need to be prepared for those episodes. Stage development in children varies from child to child and it is imperative for the counselor/pastor to understand children's level of understanding and comprehension. Papadatou and Papadatos explain,

Psychologist Maria Nagy explored the meaning of death to children of various ages. She found out that at the age 3-5, children deny that death is final. To them it is like going to sleep, or like a parent's going to work or away on brief vacation. Between 5 and 9, youngsters accept the idea that someone else has died, but usually not until the ages 10 do they understand that they themselves will die.[142]

Consoling the Dying Child

> In biblical counseling, children require counseling as they face death because they have been infected with HIV/AIDS. Land writes,

The efficiency of vertical transmission is not clearly understood yet, but studies estimate that 25% to 45% of children born to HIV-infected mothers will become infected with HIV … . In fact, due to the child's possession of passive HIV antibodies from mother, the HIV antibody test is not a reliable predictor of infection status. It is not until the child is 15 to 18 months old that a positive HIV test can demonstrate HIV infection with certainty in the absence of major infections indicative of HIV.[143]

As HIV infected children get old enough to understand their situation, they would need spiritual as well as social support. Biblical counseling for children, therefore, entails showing them God's love and care and that they would soon be united with Christ when they die. They should be encouraged to participate in the family sorrows so that they can be able face grief in the future. It is helpful for children to know about death through their pets and learn from the experience. Knowing that when they die they do not come back to life again is a good lesson.

The question is how does one counsel a dying child? The fundamental aspect of death is to teach children to cope with death or the dying. Most children will want to find the meaning in their lives and in their death. Dying is normal, is a natural phenomenon, and has to be understood that it is not a psychiatric illness or abnormal.[144] After testing, when children know they are HIV/AIDS positive, some may resort to or plan to commit suicide because they do not find the answers and the meaning in life. HIV/AIDS victims sometimes avoid pain by ending their lives. During good times, children must form alliances within the home to protect, defend, share secrets, sorrows, and happiness but when one of them dies, it creates anxiety, confusion and behavioral change.

Giving Hope to Surviving Siblings

Counseling requires an understanding of four components of human beings. Each sphere affects the other because they are interconnected. Humans share four quadrants: spiritual/intuition, emotional, intellectual, and physical.

A counselor/pastor must be familiar with human faculties and how they function in order to meet the needs of a church member regardless of age.[145]

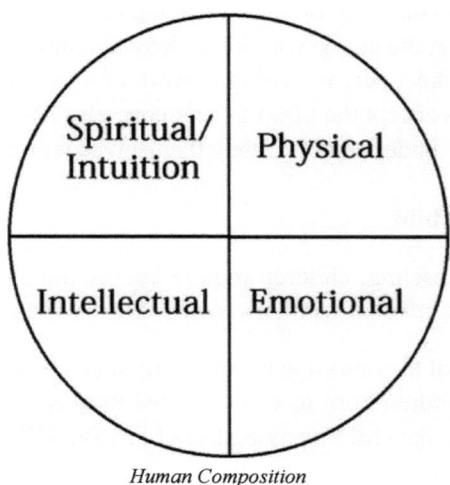

Human Composition

In biblical counseling, the four human faculties are taken into consideration. The spiritual dimension is affected when someone is going through a problem, such as HIV/AIDS. The emotional sphere of a human being is also affected when his/her spiritual life is affected by having HIV/AIDS. The physical part also goes through mechanical in- balance thus making him/her weak and unable to do certain physical work with much vigor and strength. His intellectual reasoning is also affected immensely. In biblical counseling, the counselor helps the counselee to balance the four faculties through the Scriptures. Christian parents teach their children about God, life after death, and the resurrection of those who believe in Christ (1 Cor 15:12-15 NKJV). The children develop into maturity knowing that even if they die, they will not fear death. They become aware that their parents or siblings will be with God whom they love when they die. They know that they will be reunited with their parents in the next world. "Dying children know that when they think of their mother or father they are already with the Lord."[146] Children who have been taught about Christ and what he does to believers when they die understand life after death in Christ. When children are dying, they already know that their flesh is too weak to sustain life and if they cannot eat, play, and do anything for others and for themselves, they will be ready to die. They understand the physical cannot hold to life any more but they will die with hope and confidence in God. Positive emotion develops when the child between one and six years old receives unconditional love from their parents or guardians. But they still have emotions like fear, anger, love and grief. Intellectual development is continuous, and their perceptions and critical thinking about death give them time to think about life in the past and the future even if they are dying.[147]

Praying with them and giving them hope and sharing with them the Word of God allows them to die peacefully and with confidence.

Challenges Women with HIV/AIDS Face

Women are the pillars of African homes and are known for their wisdom in advising their husbands and children; however, when crisis strikes, they are left confused, stranded, helpless, and hopeless for the future. HIV/AIDS has decimated family ties, values, resources, relationships, and hopes for the future. If the husband dies of HIV/AIDS and they are also HIV/AIDS positive, it compounds their predicaments and presents a dire future because of their lack of basic needs to provide for their children.

Land explains,

> Families with few resources and multiple problems are faced with overwhelming stress upon diagnosis of HIV. Such a diagnosis may overwhelm an already vulnerable family structure and result in a parent's relapse into drug use, abandonment by a partner/spouse, and/or emotional chaos or paralysis leading to the breakdown or dissolution of the family unit.[148]

Women, in Africa in general and in Zimbabwe in particular, are the victims of abandonment and abuse. They often develop depression, which is detrimental to their health.

Cultural Trends Expose Women to HIV/AID's Vulnerability

> The reason the rate of HIV infections for women in Africa is rising higher than men is because women are treated inferior socially, economically, and legally due to traditional and cultural trends. Dube asserts,

> Women and young girls are more often than not denied the right to property ownership, decision-making and education in patriarchal societies. They become dependent to their husbands, lovers, brothers, uncles or fathers, and are unable to fend for themselves. They have no control over their bodies and therefore are unable to insist on safer sex… Violence in the home, fueled by acceptable gender inequalities, often leaves many women afraid to call for abstinence in relationships.[149]

Although one would not agree with all of Dube's perception, it is true that the African women for centuries or for thousands of years have been undermined in their respective cultures and traditions. Men tend to dominate women's sexuality (including young girls) in Africa, which puts them at high risks. Many are raped or coerced into sexual relations because of cultural trends or for merely survival. Violence against women is rampant in Africa because of the culture. Dube writes,

> Although many women are becoming infected via their male sex partners…women are also threatened with HIV transmission through the smoking of 'crack' cocaine. Sexual favors may be exchanged for the drugs, thus exposing these women to HIV via multiple sex partners.[150]

> Women with HIV/AIDS in Zimbabwe face many challenges, especially if they have children. They struggle to take care of themselves and their children who may also be HIV/AIDS positive. They suffer from depression and stress as they become widows; not having income to support the family and to send children to school. Some women resort to prostitution or cross borders to neighboring countries to buy and sell goods; however, while doing such businesses, they are coerced into sexual relations with HIV/AIDS infected partners. Poverty also forces HIV/AIDS positive women to encourage their daughters to find partners in order to get financial support thus exposing them to child-sex workers. Ezekiel Kalipeni, Karen Flynn, and Cynthia Pope explain,

In many cases, women find themselves in economically dependent relationships with men whereby they must stay in risky situations to be able to feed themselves and, very often, their children. Young women are often married too early without regard to their potential or actual educational achievement, and are generally prevented from partaking in economically gainful activities that might lend them a semblance of empowerment. Their economic and social vulnerability is often made worse by the lack of formal education investment in them, which leaves them without access to information vital to their overall reproductive health, including but not limited to, knowledge and prevention of diseases such as AIDS.[151]

The challenges that HIV/AIDS positive women and girls face are compounded by the unavailability of antiviral drugs and medications; they do not have easy access to antiviral drugs because of the prejudice associated with the disease. Almond suggests, "In the case of this argument, the issue shifts from the interest of women to the interest of the community, so that the issue becomes: should pregnant women be treated as means to other people's ends?"[152] As far as the moral argument about the use of women is concerned, the fact is that the argument overlooks the way in which the interest of women bearing children is closely and deeply connected.[153] The biblical counselor should be aware of the discrimination that may be in force in the social structures, intentionally or unintentionally.

Some social taboos may be oppressive to women compounded by patriarchal and conservative systems that have been in place for thousands of years. The church faces a dilemma in how to confront and reset Christian teaching of equality, freedom, submission, love, fairness, and mutual respect for women in the church and society. A biblical counselor would not refer the patients to secular alternative approaches to counseling because biblical counseling offers the holistic solution to man's problem.

Microbicides an Alternative for Women to Reduce Risks of HIV/AIDS

Biblical counseling offers scriptural advice about all spiritual, social, and moral advice to all counselees seeking to find solutions about their problems. In medical fields, however, there are some alternatives offered to patients when they cannot find solutions to their problems.

New technologies that have been developed in recent years, such as microbicides, offer alternatives to women who become pregnant and are also combating HIV and sexual transmitted infections. In Christian ethics, there are still debates about whether the Christian counselor can refer his members or patients to such available alternatives. Kalipeni, Flynn, and Pope write,

For example, Sylla and Kaplan have discussed that microbicides may be a new technology that allows women to become pregnant while also combating HIV and other sexually transmitted infections. These two authors note that microbicides have the potential to revolutionize HIV prevention for women as drastically as the pill transformed women's options and protections. While microbicides will not be substitute for challenging systemic gender inequality, and first generation products are likely to be less efficacious than condoms, microbicides will increase women's power to reduce risks of HIV/AIDS. [154]

In Zimbabwe, such technological equipment are not yet available, but sooner or later they will be. Biblical counselors should be aware of these technological advancements and examine them through Scriptures to see if they are good or bad for their clients.HIV/AIDS is about life and death. It is sad to note that women have been drawn into the arena of the sex industry by poverty, marginalization, and inequality in Zimbabwean society and most of the third world countries. Kalipeni, Flynn, and Pope explain,

> The sex industry, previously considered marginal, has come to occupy a strategic and central position in the developing of international capitalism in which millions of women and children have been converted into sexual commodities through commercial sex work, wars, expansion of the tourist industry, the growth and normalization of pornography, and internationalization of arranged marriages. [155]

Integrated Relational Therapy (IRT)
as a Multimodal Therapy

> The IRT as a model of therapy is a new secular method of therapy available to omen with HIV/AIDS. This kind of treatment is used when HIV/AIDS positive women find themselves in. Counseling from a pastor or a counselor is ideal for these women and children. The model recommended by secular counselors, who would not look to Scripture to find solutions, is IRT. It is a purely humanistic kind of therapy that zeros in on self-determination and self-treatment, which is contrary to biblical counseling. Simonds explains,

Integrated Relational Therapy (IRT) is a multimodal, interactive therapy in that it draws from interpersonal, relational, cognitive-behavioral, humanistic, psychodynamic, and postmodern therapy techniques.... IRT is contextual in that the therapist chooses the treatment issues and therapy technique that most fit a given client at a given time.... IRT is a practical, contextual, integrative, and feminist model capable of addressing the needs of the wide range of diverse women who experience the heterogeneous phenomenon known as unipolar depression.[156]

This type of secular therapy treatment is not recommended, as it is an egocentric kind of therapy, but instead biblical counseling should be recommended which puts God and Scripture at the center of counseling. Biblical counseling gives hope to the individual through the Scriptures.

> In I Thessalonians 1:3, Paul writes of the 'endurance that comes from hope'. The connection between hope and endurance is one with which every counselor should be familiar... . In the Bible, 'hope' refers to a certainty. It means the expectation of an event that is sure to take place. It is certain because God has promised it.[157]

The contrast between IRT and biblical counseling is that in biblical counseling the counselee is counseled in the light of the Bible while the IRT is egocentric. It lacks the authenticity of God's voice and guidance. It is therefore not credible to the Christian faith. The IRT model respects individuals and may work for each person differently: "IRT simultaneously addresses the affective, cognitive, behavioral, and systematic issues related to depression and its recovery."[158] When counseling women with HIV/AIDS, there is a need to find a lasting solution to their depression. Biblical counseling offers credible and long lasting solutions to people's problem. Simonds continues,

> Therapy provides an opportunity to examine beliefs and behaviors that women have about relationships, to examine the way others' expectations influence the client's sense of self, and regain or strengthen connection with self. A positive relationship appears to mobilize change processes in therapy with depressed individuals.[159]

In biblical counseling, HIV/AIDS women can build their confidence, worthiness, hope, and God's assurance to restore them. They can recover from depression and be women of value and integrity. However, Simonds recounts IRT in contrast to biblical counseling, "Recovery from depression entails reclaiming the self and often transforming aspects of self and also dependence on Christ."[160]

> There is still an open debate about biblical counseling and secular counseling as therapy. The question is when can the biblical counselor refer his/her clients to medically therapeutic institutions? For example, when one's client has symptoms of schizophrenia, or when the client or member of the church is encouraged to trust in the Lord yet still suffers from mental condition.

Rational Emotive Therapy as a Model for Interventions

In contrast to biblical counseling in which the Scriptures are the source and base of counseling, Wetzel suggests a different and secular therapeutic way to counsel those who are depressed because of HIV/AIDS:

Rational Emotive Therapy is an appropriate example of such a model of interventions. Concerned with self-perception, Rational Emotion Therapy focuses on irrational cognitions. A confrontative, educational, often facetious tack is taken to help clients gain insight into their unrealistic beliefs… . Self-actualization in which efforts can also be made to actualize the ideal ego-state when feasible, by applying self-actualization principles consisting three components: the fulfillment of social needs, psychological needs, and the realization of an ideal existence as conceived by the individual.[161]

This kind of perception of counseling cannot go unchallenged. This model of counseling is humanistic in nature and starts from highlighting egocentric concerns. The theory purports that humans have the ability to become self-conscious of themselves and then in self-actualization are able to free themselves from their problems. In contrast to biblical counseling, this kind of counseling advocates self-determination, self-actualization, and the realization of ideal existence. Wetzel provides a secular therapeutic theory to human problems, and as such, one would refute such a proposition because it undermines the biblical solution. Biblical counseling by contrast is "motivated by Scriptures, founded Pre-supposition ally, upon the Scriptures, structured by the goals and objectives of the Scriptures, and developed systematically in terms of the practices and principles modeled and enjoined in the Scriptures."[162] Biblical counsel focuses on the Bible to provide all the answers to man's problem.

According to Simonds, there are five major treatment themes: assessment, safety, activation, connection and meaning. Simonds writes,

Assessment gives information we need to understand the client and her world….Safety encompasses four areas (a) a safe and facilitative therapeutic environment; (b) a safe plan for the high-risk client; (c) a zone of safety for the seriously depressed or low-functioning client; and (d) safe and secure life circumstances….
Activation refers to an attitude that encompasses four areas: (a) state of mind (from passive acceptance to active commitment); (b) daily life… . Activation represents empowerment for the depressed woman… . Connection to (a) a mutually empathic connection between client and therapist, (b) the client's connection with her own authentic, inner experience, and (c) healthy, authentic connection with others. Meaning, from the work of connection flows a transformation of meaning structures

from negative, rigid, narrow, and fixated to positive, flexible broadened, and receptive.[163]

The five elements of therapy are interconnected to each other as a model of counseling. The client/patient can be treated with the therapy using fivemajor treatment themes.[164]

Women with HIV/AIDS in Zimbabwe face difficult challenges and sometimes are left alone with their children to defend, feed, educate, dress, and to meet all their needs and their children's needs. The church gives hope to the hopeless, counsels the widows and orphans, and meets needs according to the teaching of the Scriptures. Simonds' model of counseling, a multidimensional model, is simple to understand and implement, but it is more humanistic and does not direct the client to trust God and to depend on His Scripture.

Counseling HIV/AIDS Church Members with Suicidal Thoughts

Human behavior is very complex and hard to understand. King Solomon wrote about the vanity of life: "The words of the Preacher, the son of David, King in Jerusalem. Vanity of vanities, saith the Preacher, vanity of vanities; all is vanity" (Eccl 1:1-2 KJV).

Life becomes vanity, i.e. meaningless, when hope is gone. When a person finds out that he/she is HIV/AIDS positive, after HIV/AIDS testing and after going through the process 76of pre- counseling and post-counseling, his/her worldview changes drastically and losehope. Life becomes meaningless as they face an unpredictable future with misery. The person is filled with anxiety, fear, confusion, stress, and depression, and sometimes finds it difficult to cope with life and sometimes resort to end his/her life immediately. Suicide is one of the ways and means people with HIV/AIDS resort to end their lives. There are many ways people commit suicide because of circumstances or situations. To understand suicide, one must understand human behavior. Douglas Jacobs and Herbert N. Brown point out that there are basically four kinds of suicides:

> Altruistic suicides are literally required by society. Here, the customs or rules of the group 'demand' suicide under certain circumstances. "Egoistic" suicide occurs when the individual has too few ties with his community. Demands to live do not reach him. "Anomic" suicides are those that occur when the accustomed relationship between an individual and his society is suddenly shattered, such as the shocking, immediate loss of a loved one, a close friend, a job, or even a fortune. "Fatalistic" suicides derive from excessive regulation. Examples would be persons such as slaves or prisoners whose futures are piteously blocked.[165]

The biblical counselor must know the types of suicide that people resort to as options to end their lives. The basic understanding of suicide in the context of these four categories shows that human behavior has great influence from social, psychological, biological, and spiritual phenomena. A counselor needs to understand what may cause the client or church member to commit suicide.

Voluntary and Involuntary Suicides

Suicides are planned, calculated, and thought out behaviors, not impulsive. Suicide relates to schizophrenia, alcoholism, addiction and also paresis. "In constructing the events preceding a death by means of a 'psychological autopsy' it was concluded that suicidal behavior is often a form of communication, a cry for help' born out of pain and anguish and a plea for response."[166] At times, suicidal thoughts come to individuals without planning, but through mental sickness. There are involuntary suicide and voluntary suicide. Those who involuntarily commit suicide may do so without having an intention to kill themselves but only do so because they have been pushed to reach the highest level of social or economic reasons. In other situations, someone may love another so much that if he/she is heart-broken, he/she may commit suicide. Some may commit suicide because they want to die to appease their god (Allah) in the Muslim faith. Everstine writes, "Then there are the most tragic of those who must end their lives—the dying. They include people who have only just been told that they are being consumed by disease or old age."[167]

> Those who are HIV/AIDS positive may become hopeless and believe that their lives have come to an end and commit suicide before they get sicker. Prisoners who have been either sentenced to death or life imprisonment are also likely to commit suicide. Everstine states,

> The compulsion to do the deed carries such urgency that it creates its own reality, and within that context it can truly be considered "involuntary." The best example is that of the grand master of human motivation, Sigmund Freud himself. His recently released last diary tells how he dealt with death when, at the age of 83, he felt that it was taking too long to arrive. Finally exhausted by pain from cancer of the jaw that he had resisted so many years, he asked his doctor to give him just enough extra morphine that would end the ordeal.[168]

Sigmund Freud argued throughout his lifetime and believed that the truth about one's self would set them free, however, he finally requested to be given extra morphine so that he could die. King Saul voluntarily commanded his armor-bearer to end his life:

> The fighting grew fierce around Saul, and when the archers overtook him, they wounded him critically. Saul said to his armor-bearer, "Draw your sword and run me through, or these uncircumcised fellows will come and run me through and abuse me." (1 Sam 31:3-4 NIV)

Involuntary suicide occurs when the person does not have control of him/herself because of pain and the physician terminates his/her life with the consent of the relatives.

Voluntary suicide is when a person decides to terminate his/her life by choice.

> Suicide of the voluntary sort is the most negative of human actions because it mocks whatever means to be human. It is the most unnatural of actions because it defies the survival instinct... . It is the worst among absurd crimes because it contradicts itself.[169]

Prevention and Reversing Suicidal Thoughts

> Counseling HIV/AIDS church members with suicidal thoughts is a challenging task, but it must be done quickly before the person kills him/herself. First, the counselor or pastor must discern or detect the motives. Everstine writes,

Detecting it, uncovering its causes, and acting swiftly to intervene are the skills that most clinicians possess intuitively... . Diverting suicidal ideation with other reframing therapy that seeks to achieve and rest on three guiding principles: diagnosis, diagnosis, diagnosis.[170]

Diagnosis is important because many people who commit suicide do not come for help and do not inform their counselors that they want to kill themselves. Their thoughts are usually hidden and cannot be detected easily.

> Two theories can be compared in the process of committing suicide: Stekel's theory and Freud's theory. These theories are similar but they differ with one stage. Stekel argues that the person who wants to commit suicide becomes deficient in relating to other people and thinks others should die but he/she is not able to express his/her wish in action. He asserts that anyone who wants to kill him/herself, first he/she would have thought of killing someone else and wishes someone was killed. Figure 5 illustrates the repressed superego, which leads to repressed murderous impulses that start with repressed impulse, then the feeling of guilt, and self- destruction.171[171]The guilty conscience (superego) drives someone to kill. His/her view is that if one wishes to kill someone else and fails to take the action, he/she can then commit suicide

Freud borrowed the thought from Stekel:[172]

> In this equation, Freud has inserted a "melancholic state" between the guilt feelings, as identified by Stekel, and the suicidal act. This state, melancholia, is the same as the one we call "depression." It is one of the most common forms of mental illness, and its role in the meaning of suicide.[173]

Stekel and Freud's secular theories can help to understand the emotional levels of the patient who wants to commit suicide, however, a biblical counselor uses the Bible as the main source to counsel a patient. A counselor needs to be able to detect and prevent suicides. A suicidal person is seeking to escape pain and wants to draw people's attention to show them that he/she has had a problem that was too difficult to solve. HIV/AIDS positive people go through a painful experience. Alec Roy explains,

> Suicide is best understood not so much as an unreasonable act-every suicide seems logical to the person who commits it given that person's major premises, styles of syllogizing, and constricted focus-as it is a reaction to frustrated psychological needs. A suicide is committed because of thwarted or unfulfilled needs.[174]

The common emotion in suicide is compounded by hopelessness and helplessness. If family members, the church, the community, and friends neglect the needs of people with HIV/AIDS, some resort to killing themselves to escape stigmatization, abandonment, deteriorated illness, shame, guilt, frustration, depression, and stress.

Hope in Christ and/or Medication

> HIV/AIDS victims easily lose hope and they despair. Adams asserts, "Counseling is the work of the Holy Spirit. Effecting counseling cannot be done apart from him. He is called the paraclete ('counselor') who in Christ's place came to be another counselor of the same sort that Christ had been to his disciples."[175] The Holy Spirit expects counselors to use His Word, the Holy Scriptures... . His counseling work is ordinarily performed through the ministry of this Word.[176] Adams points out that "counseling without the Scriptures can only be expected to be counseling without the Holy Spirit."[177] Christ is the hope of those who are despondent and frustrated by life without him. The scourge of HIV/AIDS leaves the victims hopeless and no longer wanting to live to their full potential. Nicolson contends,

> We want to give people with AIDS hope. But in truth they will die. Do we have no hope to offer but the opiate of heavenly bliss? No search of the Bible for a sacred word about AIDS can sidestep the resurrection. But resurrection must be understood as a present reality. Whatever the resurrection means about life after death, it has a great deal of meaning about life after AIDS, life with AIDS, and a life transformation now.[178]

The resurrection of Christ is the hope of our resurrection and restoration. With hope in Christ, still some HIV/AIDS positive people want to commit suicide and end their lives. Suicide can be preventable if the person receives biblical counseling before he/she takes his/her life. Thoughts of encouragement, advice, information, assurance and confidence on themselves and others through seeing a doctor, counselor, or relative before one commits suicide can prevent suicide. The medical community offers certain suicide preventions through medication and has proven to depress suicidal thoughts scientifically, especially the prescription of hypnotics and tranquilizers. Improved mental health services can also reduce the prevalence of suicides. Roy states, "Lithium carbonate, it is maintained, prevents relapses in the recurrent depression."[179] Medication is not the best answer to prevent suicidal thoughts; it is the last resort if counseling or psychotherapy has failed. The church must give ultimate moral, social, physical, and spiritual support to those who have conditions that can lead to a high risk of suicide. Roy concludes,

> Last, effective prevention depends not only on the efficient pharmacological and psychological treatment of the depressive patient, but also on devising a systematic policy for his after care, of course, also goes for the depressed alcoholic and other high risk patients. If suicide prevention is to be become a practicable reality, therefore, the medical and social services need to be organized so as to attain this goal.[180]

HIV/AIDS positive persons long to reduce pain and to lighten pressure. Addressing the person's perturbation, i.e., the things that are wrong in the individual's lethality will reduce suicidal thoughts. The counselor or therapist must direct the therapy to match with the individual's needs.

Counseling HIV/AIDS Orphans

Vulnerability of Orphans and Child Abuse

> HIV/AIDS has caused havoc, frustration, disunity, and disintegration of families, and has brought misery, hopelessness, helplessness, and confusion on the definition of a family. In Africa in general, and in Zimbabwe in particular, an ideal family includes a mother and a father with or without children. It is still defined as a family if the father, who is the head of the household, dies and leaves his wife and children behind. Because of the HIV/AIDS epidemic, the definition of a family has been distorted in Zimbabwe. Many times, both parents die, and siblings carry on living in the house or homestead with the family name. It becomes awkward to see children heading to homes without their fathers and mothers: this is the result of HIV/AIDS in the lives of young children. Dale Hanson Bourke writes,

According to the 2011 report of UNAIDS, there are 16.6 million children worldwide who are orphaned due to AIDS. The number is so high because HIV-infected people are typically of childbearing age. Women are often infected by their husbands and may find out they are infected only after giving birth to a child who is obviously sick. [181]

Orphans are at high risk of child abuse, child labor, dropping out of school, and not having a bright future. Bourke points out,

> Children may lose one parent to AIDS and continue to live with the other, or they may be abandoned or sent to live with relatives because a parent is too ill to care for them... . The vast majority of AIDS orphans live in Africa, where children are traditionally cared for by relatives. Sometimes grandparents are caring for their grandchildren after their sons and daughters have died. Increasingly, there are households where the oldest sister or brother cares for the younger children.[182]

In biblical counseling, children are counseled to cope with losing their parent(s) to AIDS. The Christian counselor prays with them and assures them that Christ is the hope for them all and encourages them to put their trust in Christ.

Helping Children with Traumatic Stress

> With the loss of one or both parents to AIDS, children usually go through traumatic distress. They are full of anxiety and unanswered questions. They have the capacity and ability to cope with stress if they can be helped to face the challenges. Anthony and Chiland contend,

> Some stimulant situations, such as abrupt changes of location, darkness, aloneness, and separation are not intrinsically dangerous, and often turn out not to have been dangerous except to the mind of the individual. Ethological work has suggested that humans, like animals, are genetically programmed to respond to a wide variety of circumstances with anxiety and appreciation, and then resort to certain safety measures.[183]

In the early development stage, every child develops attachment to their parents and siblings. Children develop their personalities based on sameness, and oneness to their parents and their siblings and also how they are treated and treat each other. However, when there is detachment from the parents, they develop mechanisms for defense and adapt to new environments and to new guardians. The children are affected for life in the process of change. They lose their identity and struggle to fit in the new environment. Anthony and Chiland write, "Identity develops through all the early stages of life when the child is first recognized, given a name, and or feels that he or she is an individual."[184]

The counselor should fully understand child development progression for children who are facing challenges in life because they do not have parents to come along them to learn, seek refuge, or security. The counselor needs to be at the level of the child's perception, understanding, and worldview without which one can miss the mark.

Children who become the head of their homes are forced to drop out of school so that they can take care of their siblings, clean their homes, garden, cook, and provide for their siblings, which becomes a traumatic experience. Child-headed households are led by children of all ages, ranging from nine to fifteen years. Children face many challenges including being bullied at school because of their poverty and dropping out of school in order to fend for their siblings and themselves. Bourke explains,

> Part of the confusion arises because children are not identified publicly as AIDS orphans since they stigmatizes them and the families who care for them. African culture has never accepted the concept of orphanages because there is a strong tradition of caring for the children of relatives or friends. But as the cost of caring for many children proves overwhelming, more child-headed households are springing up.[185]

The community expects them to work hard to support their siblings but most of the time their peers despise and laugh at them because of being the children of HIV/AIDS victims. Samuels explains,

> During the first year, consistent, dependable care leads to a basic sense of trust....
> The basic sense of trust leads to attachment to the caregiver (usually the mother). Attachment is an affection tie between two specific people, which binds them together in space and endures over time.[186]

Samuels explains that children develop in stages, in their first year they begin to depend on whoever feeds, teaches, and trains them. Within two years, they start an attachment to the caregiver. The early years are crucial for children's development. If they are orphaned when they are still young.

The Church Becomes a New Family

> At the age of nine to twelve, if a child is left without a parent and he/she is forced by circumstances to head the household, it usually leads to traumatic experiences. The child develops anxiety and fear. Shirley states, "The frustration—aggression model is one theory of aggressive behavior that hypothesizes that frustration and leads to anger."[187]

The counselor/pastor should meet them at their point of need and at their level of their understanding to affirm, encourage, teach, comfort, and assure them of the support. Samuels writes,

> The society in which children live (including family, school, religion, and society as a whole) has certain expectations for individuals to live to expectations. The expectation in most societies requires that children be assertive, intelligent, competitive, as well as cooperative, athletic, physically, attractive, healthy, independent, and socially gregarious but that demand puts pressure on individual children who do not live up to the standards.[188]

Children that head their households feel that they are not loved by society. Samuels continues, "Deviance from expected norms can lead to emotional behaviors that are used to defend against the pain of 'not good enough'" [189]These children feel inferior and dejected and develop low self- esteem. The church must assimilate orphans into programs that help them rise up to be the children God created them to be. They also face academic challenges. Riese explains,

> Because of their isolated status in society, many of them have been largely inaccessible for observation and treatment... . A valid evaluation of their actual limitations in being able to absorb academic knowledge and of their ability to benefit from new experience presents a considerable challenge to the therapist and educator.[190]

The challenges and competition that orphans face are beyond their capabilities because they are sidelined and prejudiced. Losing a parent or both parents and then acting as a parent is a tragic experience as they are not meant to act like parents while they are children. Riese concludes, "To children who are sensitized by an unending series of disconcerting experience, with gratification delayed or denied, the future is a most uncertain thing and is usually discounted."[191] Riese's assertion summarizes the predicaments children can face in the future if left alone without guidance for their future.

Conclusion

Counseling the victims of HIV/ADS in light of the Scriptures is a fundamental phenomenon that requires knowledge of the Scriptures and ability to apply it to the lives of those people. Nicolson writes,

> Although AIDS and HIV were quite unknown in Bible times, and although our context is so different, we do find in all sorts of ways that infection on the Bible helps us see AIDS and people with AIDS in a different way from before. The dialogue between text and present context bring new light to both the text and the situation in which we find ourselves.[192]

The biblical response to HIV/AIDS calls for an awakening of the church and biblical counselors to be geared to face this disease headlong for prevention. A change of sexual behavior and counseling for those who are stressed and have depression because of HIV/AIDS will usher in a new century with an AIDS-free generation. Interpersonal support is important to people living with HIV/AIDS. Biblical counseling, in the light of the Bible, stands out as the best method of counseling men, women, and children compared to other methods in this chapter. The counselees are offered biblical solutions to HIV/AIDS, depression, suicidal thoughts, and HIV/AIDS stigma, and women with HIV/AIDS and children orphaned by HIV/AIDS are helped. Biblical counseling points people to Christ's everlasting hope through the Bible, God's Word.

CHAPTER 4

THEORETICAL AND PRACTICAL RESPONSE TO HIV/AIDS THROUGH BIBLICAL COUNSELING

The chapter discusses the theoretical and practical implications of HIV/AIDS and the biblical response. It also discusses the transmission of the disease, strategies to combat the spread of the disease, and forgiveness of the suspected individuals. The church should strategically design programs to train, counsel, and educate church members about HIV/AIDS. The church has to have a voice in the community about the gospel of peace, hope, and salvation in Christ. The church should be in a position to answer questions asked by atheists about life after death.

The chapter discusses models to combat the spread of HIV/AIDS, through biblical counseling. The chapter includes a description of the International Christian Leadership Development and Counseling Institute, Inc. (ICLDCIM), which will be implemented in Zimbabwe.[193] The Institute will be the arm of the church, International Fellowship Baptist Church (IFBC), to reach out to and counsel HIV/AIDS victims as a tool for evangelism.

The Value of Knowing One's HIV/AIDS Status

Pre-Counseling and Post-Counseling

As a model to combat the spread of HIV/AIDS, pre and post-counseling is one of the means to help those with the disease. Members of the church who seek to be tested for HIV/AIDS need to be knowledgeable and equipped to handle their emotions, actions, and decisions in order to avoid stress, depression, and suicidal thoughts. The church should encourage the members to get HIV/AIDS testing in order to make informed decisions for their lives. To live without the knowledge of one's HIV/AIDS status, especially in Zimbabwe, is a disastrous situation. HIV/AIDS affects families in their normal life. It affects those with HIV/AIDS in their own perception about themselves and how they are perceived by others in the church and society. Hoffman contends,

> This worldwide pandemic has enormous implications for the health and psychosocial well-being of individuals, their family structures, and their community structures, for the delivery of psychosocial and medical services, and responses by government agencies.[194]

Hoffman asserts that the impact of HIV/AIDS has caused and continues to impact the lives of the families.

In pre-counseling, the counselor sits down with the counselee who is seeking to know his/her HIV/AIDS status before testing. In post-counseling, the counselee has completed the HIV/AIDS testing and is ready to receive the results. Post-counseling has some challenges especially if the counselee is HIV/AIDS positive. In the process, the counselor informs the counselee about his/her HIV/AIDS test results. If he/she is HIV/AIDS positive, the counselee is advised about how to eat and how to live a healthy life, where, when, and how antiviral drugs can be taken, and how they can help to boost immunity. If the test results are negative, the individual is given information and advised to prevent him/herself from contracting the disease.

HIV/AIDS Transmission

When one knows his/her HIV/AIDS status, the individual should begin to change his/her sexual behavioral in order to avoid further infections. The needed changes to behavior change can present challenges. Hoffman reiterates,

> First, HIV is transmitted through behaviors that are usually private and are often associated with norms and values of a subculture. Disclosing one's HIV status can reveal intimate aspects about one's life and can result in stigma and discrimination from others.[195] HIV/AIDS is not transmitted only through sexual intercourse with the infected person; some infections occur through sharing needles used by HIV/AIDS infected persons or through sharing razor blades with an infected person. In some cases, transmission can take place through pregnancy, child-mother transmissions, or through breast feeding. The majority of infections and transmissions occur through unprotected sex with an infected person. Even though there will be a stigma after disclosing HIV/AIDS status, it is important to have an action plan.

> The advantages of knowing one's HIV/AIDS status are numerous, including choosing a life-partner, knowing what to eat, taking anti-viral drugs to boost one's immunity, and planning for pregnancies. Shernoff explains,

> Since in its early phases, HIV is primarily an asymptomatic illness, many patients will present on an ambulatory basis. Ambulatory patients can be defined as such when an individual present for 'personal health services that is neither bedridden nor

currently admitted to any healthy institution. Ambulatory patients are usually responsible for the majority of their care, e.g. taking their own medication, monitoring their symptoms, and following their response to treatment.[196]

When the patients are able to take their own medication, choose their diet, and exercise without assistance, they are able to plan their lives and live as people without the disease. Church members are encouraged to know their HIV/AIDS status in order to plan ahead so that they can cope with life for some years before they become prone to other diseases that may quicken the faltering of their immune systems and die earlier than expected.

Strategies to Combat HIV/AIDS in Families, Church, and Community

Sexual Abstinence before Marriage

Sexual abstinence before marriage as a model to prevent HIV/AIDS infections is a biblical principle (Rom 12:1-2 NIV)? Changing sexual lifestyle, such as prostitution, unprotected sex, adultery, fornication, homosexuality and drug abuse promotes the decline of HIV/AIDS infections. Behavioral change can also alter the trend of sexual lifestyle. How can one change those habits and what are some strategies to combat HIV/AIDS infection in the family, church, and community? The church teaches sexual abstinence before marriage and faithfulness within marriage. Prostitution is a sin, and if one engages in the lifestyle, he/she has to stop, repent, and live a godly life if he/she is a Christian. If he/she is not a Christian, cultural norms still condemn such behaviors and practices in the society, hence it is imperative to abandon the trade and become a responsible citizen. The Bible teaches self-control and a discipline: "Therefore, I urge you, brothers, in view of God's mercy, to offer your bodies as living sacrifices, holy and pleasing to God-this is your spiritual act of worship" (Rom 12:1 NIV).

HIV/AIDS: Anti-Viral Drugs

For those already infected with HIV/AIDS, anti-viral drugs are used to combat the spread of HIV/AIDS. Scientists have discovered that anti-viral drugs can boost the immune system. Jager points out,

> Retrovirus, of which HIV is one, is situated as to build their genetic information into the gene bank of cell. When there is a failure to kill the virus or eliminate it from the body, replication of the virus should be arrested by a drug (virus stasis) or it should be prevented from attacking cells.[197]

The HIV/AIDS patients must take heed of the important information about the drugs they use. Jager continues, "With this type of management an attempt should be made, by means of a drug, a hormone, or some other kind of therapy, to step up the body's immune function and perhaps to induce the immune system to recreate the cells destroyed by the virus."[198] As there is no cure for HIV/AIDS, prevention programs must be administered in order to minimize the spread of the disease.

The use of the sterile disposable needles prevents the infection, and the use of condoms has been found to be effective when used. When one is infected with HIV/AIDS, it affects the family, church, and community. Can the challenges of HIV/AIDS in the family, church or community be avoided? Hoffman writes, "Each person who is infected, each person who dies, is someone's daughter, someone's sister or brother, someone's husband or wife, mother or father, friend and loved one. We hide from this reality as a way to avoid feeling the pain."[199] Like the relationship among family members, the church community is interconnected. The support and care from the triangular relationship can be used as a preventative measure against the spread of HIV/AIDS. Some preventative measures to curb the spread of HIV/AIDS are sexual abstinence before marriage, faithfulness within marriage, avoiding the use sharing needles or razor blades as an infected person, and preventing mother-to-child transmission through blood transfusion or breast milk.

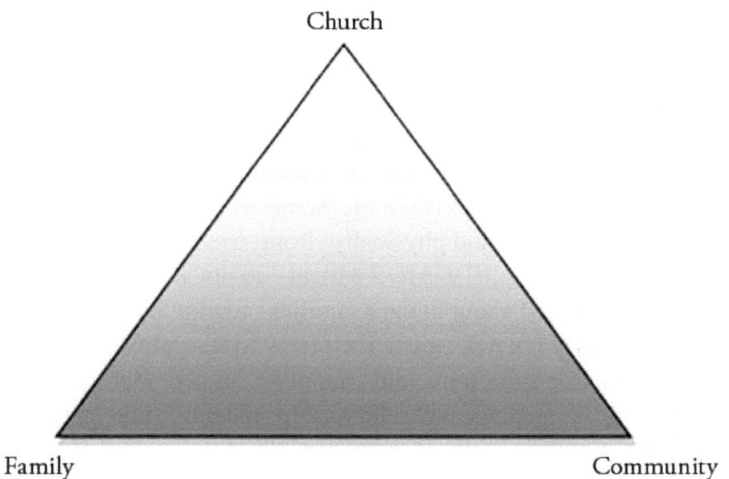

Triangular relationship between the family, the church, and Community

The relationship between the family and church is entwined in an African context. The family makes the church because the church is composed of families. When the family is healthy, so is the church. The family and community are also inseparable. An African proverb states, "I am because we are and we are because I am." The proverb means that a person and his/her personality, character, and behavior are shaped and influenced by the community. The character, personality, and behavior of a person are formed by the influence, advice, and teachings of the community. The family has great influence on an individual's behavior, but the community and family is not held accountable when an individual misbehaves and when the individual becomes the misfit of the family and community. The church is regarded as the builder of good, moral, and spiritual excellence of every person who is a member.

When HIV/AIDS was discovered in the late 1980s, it was taboo for any person to contract the disease. Dortzbach and Long explain,

> In the early years of the epidemic, the international AIDS conference convened every year to share and debate the most recent advances in the molecular configurations and DNA of the virus that cause AIDS... . The virus seemed to be contained within the homosexual community and pockets of cities.[200]

Anyone who was discovered to have contracted the disease was either excommunicated or stigmatized until they left the church on their own. Dortzbach and Long continue, "Many people felt immune ... Christians didn't bother to get involved. In North America we thought it was a gay disease-a justifiable gay disease, in fact, that showed the consequences of sexual sin."[201] The early perception about the existence of HIV/AIDS was not clear and unknown, in general. Dortzbach and Long write, "In fact, the virus copies itself, disguises itself and, with new configurations viral parts, strengthens itself to do the sinister work of destroying the very system the body uses to defend itself from such invasions."[202] The HIV/AIDS still carries a stigma that and infected persons wrestle with the choice of disclosing their HIV/AIDS status.

Although the stigma against HIV/AIDS can make it difficult for diagnosed people to maintain close relationships, interpersonal support is very important. When a person has been infected by the disease, there is fear of rejection and abandonment. Some fear infecting others, hence they resort to isolation. Some who are infected with HIV/AIDS distance themselves emotionally and physically from friends, families, and churches to avoid stigmatization. Many HIV/AIDS patients do not want to disclose their status fearing that they may be talked about in their families, workplaces, schools and in the church. They would rather not tell about their HIV/AIDS status for fear of the stigma, until the disease has visible symptoms and cannot be hidden. Both psychological and physical support can foster openness and relationships but until someone sees the support he/she needs, one is not willing to disclose his/her HIV/AIDS status. Hoffman writes,

> The studies that have been reviewed show an important link between social support, physical and psychological well-being. However, it is not clear whether social support leads to psychological well-being and consequently to better health, or if better psychological and physical well-being lead to higher levels of social support.[203]

Social support for those with HIV/AIDS must be enhanced by the church and the community in order to allow the victims to willingly disclose their HIV/AIDS status and get help, in one way or another.

Religious and spiritual support is foundational in dealing with those that have HIV/AIDS. Support from the church in the form of prayer, counseling, church attendance, and support groups plays an important role in providing spiritual nourishment. Hoffman asserts, "Examples of community, medical, and psychological services that can serve as sources of social support include support groups, buddy programs, housing programs, hospice care, AIDS hotlines, and legal assistance."[204] Both the church and community can work together to support and care for HIV/AIDS positive people in their communities. In Africa in general, healing and therapy is left to the African traditional healers of the society. There have been many misconceptions as to the origin and cure of HIV/AIDS. Some African traditionalists believe the disease is associated with the disgruntled spirits and spiritual mediums that have been invaded by foreigners. Unfortunately, HIV/AIDS positive patients in Zimbabwe and in African in general have been cheated repeatedly with false propositions that traditional healers can cure the disease and/or that they can reverse symptoms. However, people continue to seek medication from self-proclaimed healers. Sullivan propounds,

> Healing combines psychology, psychotherapy, religion, and herbal medication. The healing ceremonies involve confession, atonement, and forgiveness…. Current scholarship and health care planning are increasingly concerned with the fate of the individuals and cohorts groups in settings where this customary procedure of looking for health in society and other therapeutic support in one's primary social group may be inoperative for either temporary or permanent reasons.[205]

Health care programs to help HIV/AIDS positive people cope with the disease give victims a chance to adjust to normal life. In Africa in particular, the influence of African traditional health concepts and values are highly regarded and considered to be better than professional medicine in Africa. African traditional healers have been highly respected for healing complex diseases until recently when professional medicine took over. In the beginning of the AIDS discovery, they African traditional healers claimed to be able to cure AIDS. But it proved that they were dealing with the symptoms only not killing the AIDS virus.

Biblical Forgiveness

HIV/AIDS positive patients have been bruised and hurt by their families, the church, and the communities because of being stigmatized. When a person has HIV/AIDS, he/she may have depression because of constantly thinking about the progression of the disease in the body and the stigma associated with it. In biblical counseling, a counselee is asked to forgive those who may have contributed to having him/her contract the disease. Christians forgive because God forgave: "Get rid of all bitterness, rage, and anger, brawling and slander, along with every form of malice. Be kind and compassionate to one another, forgiving each other, just as Christ God forgave you" (Eph. 4:31-32 NIV). To forgive is to let go, to clean the slate, to pardon and to cancel a debt. By forgiving, one restores relationships and reconciliation. It is an act of love as Christ loves: "So watch yourself. If your brother sins, rebuke him, and if he repents, forgive him. If he sin against you seven times in a day, and seven times comes back to you and ask, 'I repent,' forgive him" (Luke 17:3-4 NIV). Christ gave all the reasons to forgive, because God forgives.

Forgiving is God's standard to show love to His people. However, forgiving is a great challenge to human beings because it is not natural to forgive. The counselor encourages the counselee as a Christian to forgive whoever may have transmitted HIV/AIDS to him/her. Even if one gets HIV/AIDS, forgiveness is unlimited according to the (Luke 17:3-4 NIV). Dortzbach and Long set a very interesting analogy:

> AIDS haunts the pathways of life, diverting them to death. God graciously gave men and women the gift of sexual expression as the most intimate celebration of life in relationship; it is also joyful collaboration with him in creating new life. AIDS makes sexual expression a channel of death.[206]

God created Adam and Eve to enjoy intimacy with each other. Marriage is a solemn union that brings a couple to mutual agreement, respect, and love for one another. Dortzbach and Long write, "Why AIDS easily catalyzes an ethical debate? We no longer see leprosy as the setting for moral contest... . Yet these other diseases don't generate much moral discussion."[207] HIV/AIDS generates debate about how it is transmitted and who gets it. It is most frequently transmitted through sex with an infected person. If people can change their behaviors sexually, have self- control, have protected sex, and fear God, HIV/AIDS spread will decline. In the same vein, for those who have been infected and are suffering and dying from the disease, the church needs to care and support them. Dortzbach and Long write,

> Jesus calls us to be compassionate, intentional involvement in the lives of people around us who are suffering, stigmatized or marginalized... . Jesus engaged compassionately and authentically with the woman at the well, drawing her into meaningful dialogue and addressing her primary need for living water.[208]

Members of the church with HIV/AIDS need teaching on forgiveness. They should be able to forgive themselves and others. Peter asked Jesus, "Lord, how many times shall I forgive my brother when he sins against me? Up seven times?" Jesus answered, "I tell you, not seven times, but seventy-seven times" (Matt 18:21-22 NIV). One must forgive as many times as one is sinned against. Christ taught about forgiveness: "For if you forgive men when they sin against you, your heavenly Father will also forgive you. But if you do not forgive men their sins, your Father will not forgive your sins" (Matt 14:6 NIV). Forgiveness is part of a Christian life.

Dube writes, "HIV/AIDS raises many complicated and unresolved ethical issues related to prevention; the provision of quality care; access to affordable treatment; stigma and discrimination."[209] Forgiveness begins with repentance, then forgiveness, reconciliation and

The impact of HIV/AIDS has "shattered the walls" of our souls, families, communities, countries, and continents. So, the 'come let us rebuild' is timely, relevant, and of crucial importance. We must develop a theology of rebuilding our broken societies, bodies, and spirits.[210]

Rebuilding families starts with forgiveness. The wrongs people have done against each other and the process to forgive has to be carefully structured in order to be effective and have impact both to the one who forgives and those who need to be forgiven.

Confronting HIV/AIDS Stigma and Shame

Confronting HIV/AIDS stigma as model to help those with HIV/AIDS to cope with shame and prejudice is a biblical mandate as the church supports and cares for such people. Helping church members with HIV/AIDS to overcome stigma and shame entails formidable strength and encouragement. Shernoff explains, "Other treatment plans depend on the individual's needs which might include goals about vocational or educational needs, family, relationships, treatment of depression or other psychiatric illness, and the need to deal with some issues from the past." 211[211]The patient must accept the fact that he/she HIV/AIDS positive. Shernoffs points out, "Secrets are the enemy of recovery. However, revealing the information about HIV status can be difficult and traumatic. Discrimination, fear, and rejection run rampant in many areas where someone might reveal his/her HIV status."[212]

Because of HIV/AIDS stigma and shame, the victims may develop depression. To avert episodes of depression, reading the Scriptures for soul care is fundamental and also health measures will help. Johnson and Hayes state, "A positive health agenda should also emphasize positive health behaviors and practices, such as diet, exercise, sleep, relaxation, and leisure, all of which are important to address depression."[213]The positive health agenda can facilitate change in behavior and lifestyle. Coyle and Muir reiterate, "The Gospel of Mark characterizes the healings as deliverance or salvation. These healing accounts draw attention both to Jesus, who is God's saving agent, and the afflicted persons."[214] Healing can be physical as well as spiritual. Jesus heals through restoration of physical ailments as well as through saving the soul.

Counseling HIV/AIDS Positive Church Members

In biblical counseling, the counselor focuses on pointing the patient to the

Scriptures and helping him/her to understand their situation in the light of the Bible. Both secular sectors and churches have increased awareness and campaign programs to prevent further HIV/AIDS infections. Earl E. Shelp and Ronald H Sunderland write,

Much has changed in our lives since 1981. Our scholarly and pastoral interests have centered on HIV/AIDS. Most of our time is committed to learning about HIV/AIDS, developing specialized AIDS ministries, and reporting on our work in journals and books.[215]

The most powerful way by which the awareness of HIV/AIDS is achieved is when a family member or friend discloses his/her status concerning the infection with the disease. Shelp and Sunderland explain,

> Epidemics do not occur in a vacuum. They take place in a social context. The church is part of the social context of HIV/AIDS. The church has been and continues to be challenged by the specific characteristics of this epidemic to reflect on its identity and mission. The integrity and witness of the body of Christ are on the line in its collective and individual member response to the HIV/AIDS crisis particularly to people touched by HIV/AIDS. The initial failure to be a prophetic voice or a healing and comforting presence ought to be confessed and must not be perpetuated.[216]

The church, as the body of Christ, should engage in effective programs to deal with the stigma and shame connected to HIV/AIDS disease. The impact of the HIV/AIDS disease is phenomenon and demands urgent response by the church. Confronting the stigma and shame of HIV/AIDS is a challenge, and yet it must be done. In combating the HIV/AIDS stigma, first there should be educational programs designed to educate people about its transmission in order to avoid contracting the disease in the first place. Education is one of the major tools used in reducing HIV transmission. Margot Taller et al. writes,

> HIV testing provides an excellent opportunity for the physician or counselor to educate and offer advice to the client or patient with respect to HIV infection. Such education is an important part of pre-testing counseling and serves to help prevent the transmission of HIV. The counseling and educational process provides information about the virus, the disease it produces, routes of transmission, and methods of reducing risks.[217]

The basis of counseling and education starts with an accurate medical history. Counselors initiate and probe the client's or a patient's willingness for voluntary testing. God calls the church to not only be an agent of change through education, but also through compassion. Taller et al., states,

> God calls us to be prophetic where there is injustice and suffering. God gives us the gift of ears to listen, perhaps more so in this time than ever before. We listen more than we expound. God calls the church to take care of HIV/ AIDS persons and to be supportive.[218]

In the same vein, psycho-social and bioethical issues, caregiver/care-receiver relationships, communication skills, and grief management are fundamental in pastoral care and counseling. Taller et al., explains,

> If the test is positive, a definitive test known as the Western Blot will then be performed for final confirmation. The HIV antibody will be present in one's blood as soon as six weeks after the initial contact with the virus and up to fourteen months after the initial exposure to Virus (HIV Testing and Risk Assessment).[219]

> The church has been entrusted by Christ to give soul care to orphans, widows, the destitute, the sick, and the needy. The church is to care for the covenant which God initiated through Christ. Helen Hayes and Cornelius Van der Poel write, "The church cares best for God's covenant when it liberates people to grow with God in all dimensions of their lives... . Such a broadening of the scope of pastoral care is consistent with the holistic view of ministry."[220] Pastoral care counseling is in the intrapersonal, interpersonal, and communal-societal level. The counseling includes psychotherapy by nature because it enables the counselor to interact with the counselee in order to come to a permanent solution to the problem. Robert J. Perilli explains,

When a person has AIDS the pastoral counselor or pastoral caregiver has a unique opportunity to interact with not only that person but the entire family. The church offers multiple points of entry into the family-probably more so than any other system.[221]

> Before one works with a family or the persons with HIV/AIDS, the pastoral counselor or caregiver must deal with his/her own fears, which could include homophobia, fear of death, and fear of contamination. Betty Clare Moffat writes,

AIDS can be healed when the patient stops being a victim of his past and takes full and total responsible for his present situation and through that total commitment, creates the future he/she wants... . AIDS can be a catalyst that brings a family together, but again, every family member is responsible for his own actions or feelings.[222]

Family members have great part to play in the healing and counseling the HIV/AIDS patient. Immediate family members know and understand their relative and can relate well with him/her without prejudice and suspensions. Pastoral ministry with the family with AIDS victim is one of the most important ways to fulfill the mandate of the church.

Kava states,

> The field of family systems therapy creates a necessary option for pastoral intervention with families. From this perspective, the family system is regarded as a living entity in itself. The perceptions of individual family members point to the larger picture in which can be seen the interactions of the family system. Tracking and in turn re-shaping (re- framing) these family system patterns creates new possibilities for family interaction.[223]

> The counselor encourages and guides the person with HIV/AIDS to cope with the disease. Kavar writes, "The pastoral minister providing care in the context of AIDS and must maintain a certain awareness of the breadth of family experience shared by those most at risk to the syndrome."[224] Counseling is one of the fundamental instruments used by the church and society to care for the infected and affected by HIV/AIDS pandemic. There is a need to understand in-depth feelings of the victims in the pastoral care offered to the infected persons. It is also important to be aware of personal feelings, values, and moral ethics in order to avoid conflicts with the counselees. Kirkpatrick propounds, "At all times careers must be non-judgmental listeners who hear, who feel and yet who are positive and honest with this person about each stage of the illness."[225]

> The biblical counselor empathizes with the counselee about his/her situation and then gives hope in Christ. In his perception, Kirkpatrick alludes, "The minister comes (as do other careers) to the pastoral situation as a person rich in the kind of faith, hope and love that nourishes one's ability to grow into mystery of shared compassion and allows for the mutual embrace of sufferer and career alike."[226] The goal of biblicalcounseling the infected person is to bring the patient to a saving knowledge of Jesus and for the person's heart to change by God's grace. The patient gradually begins the healing process as he/she learns the consequences of the disease and begins to depend on Christ. The rapport between the counselor and the counselee is fundamental in opening up and finding the lasting solutions to the counselee. Hoffman writes, "Therapeutic relationships flourish when the counselor and client develop a strong therapeutic alliance. Interpersonal aspects of the relationship focus on the interplay between the counselor and the client."[227]

Counseling is conducted as if the client has many more years to live ahead with many dreams, hopes, faith, and aspirations. Interventions include working through emotions, understanding what it means to have HIV disease, and living positively. Self-disclosure is one of the most important healing therapeutic tools available, which can serve anxiety and needs. To counsel an HIV/AIDS patient, one needs some basic skills that are fundamental to both the counselor and the counselee. The counselor must know the client's disease, not as physician, but as a professional counselor. Ivey and Gluckstern have written on the basic skills of counseling:

Listening is basic skill and greatest gift to give out and indicates caring. Interviewing, counseling and therapy is the ability to experience life through another person's eyes, ears and feelings. The central theme of Basic Attending skills is listening, listen, listen and listen, then listen some more before acting or giving advice.[228]

The caregivers make themselves available to give moral, emotional, physical and psychological support to members of the church who are HIV/AIDS positive. With God's help through the Holy Spirit and other people, the counselee can find comfort, consolation, and hope in Christ and thereby live a full life even if he/she HIV/AIDS positive.

Conclusion

Pre-counseling gives the counselee information about the results that he/she will receive. In preparing the counselee for the HIV/AIDS results, the counselor goes through the process with the counselee about his/her choices in life after knowing his/her HIV/AIDS status. In post- counseling, the counselee has completed the HIV/AIDS testing and is ready to receive the results. When one knows his/her HIV/AIDS status, he/she may begin to be aware of his/her lifestyle and choices to make about sexual behavioral change. For those already infected with HIV/AIDS, anti-viral drugs may be used to combat the spread of HIV/AIDS. Interpersonal support is very important to people with HIV/AIDS. The support is helpful to keep connectedness with family members, the church, and the community.

This chapter discussed the transmission of HIV/AIDS through casual and unprotected sex, blood transfusion, breast-feeding, unsterilized needles, and using razor blade used by the infected person. It discussed the strategies used to combat the spread of HIV/AIDS. In the same vein, the chapter discusses anti-viral drugs which decrease the replication of the virus in the body of the infected person. The chapter expounded on the biblical forgives that starts with knowing God's forgiveness of oneself and then moves to others who may have contributed in the process of the infection. It captured practical ways to help those infected with HIV/AIDS. The chapter concludes with how to confront the stigma and shame associated with HIV/AIDS and the basic skills necessary for counselors to use when counseling HIV/AIDS positive church members.

CHAPTER 5

RESEARCH IMPLICATIONS, APPLICATIONS AND FURTHER RESEARCH

A biblical response to HIV/AIDS positive people through biblical counseling creates opportunities for the church to serve people with Christ's love. The idea that the church should be making a difference in the lives of HIV/AIDS positive people is fundamental in accordance with the Scriptures. Biblical counseling for HIV/AIDS positive members should impact the value system in which the trend for some years has been to marginalize those who are infected by the disease. The purpose of this thesis was to perform a comparative analysis of leprosy and HIV/AIDS stigma and the biblical response through counseling. The thesis intended to equip pastors and Christian leaders to biblically respond to the HIV/AIDS pandemic in the church and beyond. This thesis created intentional strategies to enable the church and its leadership to respond to HIV/AIDS persons through counseling and by giving the victims the tools to protect themselves and others and prevent the spread of HIV/AIDS. This chapter analyzes, evaluates and gives my personal reflections about this thesis.

Research Implications

The purpose of this thesis was to contrast leprosy with the HIV/AIDS stigma and the biblical response to lepers in Israel with the response to HIV/AIDS positive people in the church. The two diseases have similar stigma and the negative responses to each had/have disastrous effects on the victims. The traditional and cultural response to lepers in Israel was devastating to the victims. Similarly, the church's religious response to HIV/AIDS positive people has been disastrous to the victims. Chapter 2 of this thesis analyzed leprosy in Israel in the Old Testament and discussed how the Israelites responded to and treated lepers. The example of Naaman's leprosy and how he was cleansed from the disease was discussed. The restoration of the unclean lepers into the society was examined through Leviticus 13:12-13 NKJV. Second Kings 7:3-20 NKJV was also examined to display how the Israelites treated those who were infected with leprosy; they threw them out of the camp and left them to die.

In the New Testament, however, Jesus Christ brought a new paradigm for thinking about and treating lepers. He showed his people to treat outcasts with love. In Luke 17:12-19 NKJV, Jesus healed the ten lepers. Jesus also showed how to respond to the lepers who were ostracized from society in Luke 10:27-30 NKJV. Chapter 2 also includes practical responses to HIV/AIDS through love, encouragement, giving, healing, helping, and mercy extended by the ministry of Christ to the downcasts of society. Chapter 2 concluded by calling for a powerful response from the church: to embrace HIV/AIDS positive people in the church, extending love, forgiveness, reconciliation, and restoration through the blood of Christ. Chapter 2, "The Biblical and Theological Foundations for Counseling HIV/AIDS," sought to provide the best tools to be used by all churches and Christians to respond to those who are broken and hurting through counseling.

Jesus, in His own counsel, embodies all human suffering and all human healing. He came to demonstrate a new approach to human treatment in forgiveness, love, encouragement, and reconciliation, regardless of a person's situation or predicament. The church is to carry the message of love, forgiveness, hope, reconciliation, discipline, self-control, kindness, long suffering, patience, soberness, purity and repentance. Jesus is the epicenter of all the virtues humanity needs.

Chapter 3 discussed the social response to HIV/AIDS through biblical counseling. The synopsis of the chapter gives vital information about HIV/AIDS and the social stigma that enhances stress and depression, suicidal thoughts, and the suffering of children and widows. In response to stress and depression, the chapter evaluated various methods to meet needs, such as Rational Emotional Therapy as a model for interventions, redirecting the counselee to Christ, sexual behavioral change, change of attitude, heart, and action toward HIV/AIDS, responsibility toward one another, repentance, and forgiveness. The chapter also discussed counseling children with HIV/AIDS by giving them hope in Christ in the midst of frustration, despondence, and facing death.

Chapter 3 concluded with a discussion of women in Africa and in Zimbabwe in particular who suffer from cultural trends that expose them to HIV/AIDS. Social taboos oppress women and are compounded by patriarchal and conservative systems. Women with HIV/AIDS who are being counseled may be given microbicides as alternative to reduce the risks of contracting HIV/AIDS. Microbicides stand as a means to transform women's options and offer protection against the contraction of HIV/AIDS. However, in evaluating alternatives, I found some discrepancies in the alternatives and I recommend reliance on Scripture as the best source for reference. Although the alternatives are debatable, one wound evaluate further the suggestion that while microbicides are not a substitute for challenging systemic gender inequality, they increase women's power to reduce the risk of HIV/AIDS. Further research should be conducted to see if it does not conflict with Christian ethics.

Chapter 4 detailed the theoretical and practical response to HIV/AIDS through biblical counseling. Pre- and post-counseling is important in the practical ways to prevent the infection and spread of HIV/AIDS. In pre-counseling, the person is counseled before HIV/AIDS testing. It prepares the counselee to accept the results whether they positive or negative and to make some choices in the future. In post-counseling, the counselee has been tested for HIV/AIDS and is given advice and tools to move forward whether or not they have HIV/AIDS positive or negative. The common ways HIV/AIDS is transmitted include unprotected sex with an infected person, using the same drug needles as an infected person, pregnancies through mother-child transmission, and using the same razor blades as an infected person. To prevent infections, suggestions are offered in the thesis

Chapter 4 outlined practical strategies to combat HIV/AIDS in the families, church, and community. Anti-viral drugs may be used to boost the immune system. The triangular relationship between the family, the church, and the community brings a bond that is cemented by trust, responsibility, and accountability. Interpersonal support is very important for people with HIV/AIDS. Support is valuable and helpful to keep connectedness with family members, the church, and the community. Religious and spiritual support is foundational in dealing with those with HIV/AIDS. Chapter 4 also addressed the HIV/AIDS stigma that church members face at home, work, in schools, or in the community where they live. Forgiving those who may have transmitted the disease is a process of treatment with psychotherapy and dealing with emotions, anxiety, and hatred. Finally, chapter 4 explained the International Christian Leadership Development and Counseling Institute (ICLDCL) that stands as the practical implementation of counseling in response to the need for leadership development and counseling for HIV/AIDS in Zimbabwe. ICLDCL has articles of incorporation and by-laws.

Research Applications

The Origin of HIV/AIDS

The thesis offers the understanding of the possible origins of HIV/AIDS. The attempt to understand and trace the origins of HIV/AIDS is important because without an understanding of the virus and its mutation, prevention and treatment of the disease are impossible. HIV/AIDS' origin is still hypothetical, although it is believed to be traced among homosexuals. Another theory suggests that it originated from gorillas in Africa. There is no substantial evidence to authenticate the claim. If there is no understanding of the virus, about its mutation and survival, the cure of the disease will still be far off the scientific reach. However, recent research sheds a glimpse of hope. The current information depicts the strength of the fight against HIV/AIDS. Knowledge is power. Understanding the origin and the mutation of the disease gives one power to critically gauge and respond vigorously to the future of human infections and the risks.

Positive response to HIV/AIDS

This thesis has numerous strengths that have been highlighted that deserve consideration in fostering a biblical response to HIV/AIDS positive members of the church. The thesis connects leprosy stigma in Israel in the Old and New Testaments to HIV/AIDS stigma in the twenty-first century. The comparative analysis of leprosy and HIV/AIDS, in the context of Christ's response, is an example the church should adopt. Christ's approach ushers in a new method for the church in counseling and supporting members with HIV/AIDS. Supporting members will result in healthy bonds among HIV/AIDS positive members and the church. The church should provide helpful intervention programs to prevent the spread of the disease. The relationships will restore trust, openness, and honest conversation about the disease and the best ways to prevent and stop the spread of the disease.

Biblical Counseling

The thesis is that biblical counseling gives counselors an opportunity to counsel clients with a biblical approach in response to an incurable disease such as AIDS. HIV/AIDS has infected, and affected negatively, individuals, families, churches, and communities. Members of the church can receive counseling assistance for stress, depression, sexual behavioral change, repentance, forgiveness, responsibility, HIV/AIDS prevention, and family unity. Counseling children with HIV/AIDS, consoling the dying child, and giving hope to the hopeless is can be achieved through biblical counseling. Counseling women with HIV/AIDS will help them to trust Christ during their difficult time and to comfort and guide their children in the fear of the Lord.

The secular therapy which are offered in counseling are secular and do not align with Christian faith in counseling. They do not offer permanent solutions to the problems HIV/AIDS victims face. Female church members with HIV/AIDS should be given adequate information about the dangers of receiving Rational Emotive Therapy as a model for interventions, Microbicides an alternative for women to reduce risks of HIV/AIDS, and Integrated Relational Therapy (IRT) as a multimodal therapy. Biblical counseling offers the best option because the counselor uses the Scriptures in light of their problems and Christian ethics.

The information contained in the thesis helps counselors to serve those with suicidal thoughts. A benefit offered by this thesis is a diminished amount of voluntary and involuntary suicides when members seek counseling. Prevention and reversing suicidal thoughts gives the thesis major strength as such counseling touches the lives of the individuals, their families, church, and community. Hope in Christ is explained in the thesis for those who want to repent, be forgiven by Christ, and restored to the body of Christ.

Practical response to HIV/AIDS

The thesis emanate from its practicality. The thesis gives the church ideas on how to handle different life situations fundamental to the curbing and prevention of new infection of HIV/AIDS. The thesis discusses sexual abstinence before marriage, anti-viral drugs, and confronting HIV/AIDS stigma and shame. Above all, the thesis has detailed the implementation of providing a biblical response to HIV/AIDS. It has not only given theoretical information about the disease, how it originated, the spread and transmission, prevention, and interventions, but it also has outlined how and when to implement the program through International Christian Leadership Development and Counseling Institute (ICLDCI) in Zimbabwe (see appendix 2). The Institute is vital and makes this thesis relevant, practical, and viable in the Zimbabwean context.

The challenges of the thesis come in three forms. First, the thesis took longer than anticipated due to some adjustments made. Its initial implementation was supposed to occur in June 2015 in Zimbabwe through the International Christian Leadership Development and Counseling Institute (ICDCI). As a result, the goals and objectives were deterred for 2015 implementations. The sourced funding is on hold until the Institute begins operating fully in January 2017.

Second, the thesis dealt with an evolving disease with on-going research. Because the cure of HIV/AIDS is not yet discovered, it was difficult to understand the nature and the mutation of the disease and how to deal with it. The thesis did not address all practical measures that can be employed and implemented in order to prevent HIV/AIDS. The biblical response to HIV/AIDS employs moral and ethical decisions that may jeopardize marriages, especially to those who are not married to Christians. The thesis did not discuss how church members of the church could front such challenges. Third, the thesis did not discuss strategic planning and open conversation with the church members that is necessary for the church to participate in the prevention and intervention against HIV/AIDS infections. However, the weaknesses of the thesis were overridden by the massive strengths of the thesis.

Further Research

Research on HIV/AIDS disease and the biblical response to it is wide and deep; therefore, further research may go deeper and further. HIV/AIDS is and continues to be complex to deal with. Its origin, mutation, nature, weaknesses, and circle continue to baffle scientists. Hypotheses about its origin and nature have shed some glimpses of light. Dugas was found to be the man who contracted HIV in the jungle of Cameroon though contact with chimps and brought it to North America. In *The Chimp and the River: How AIDS Emerged from an African Rain Forest*, Quammen asserts,

Dugas, through his extensive travels and unrepentant, unprotected sex even after he was diagnosed, undoubtedly helped spread AIDS. But was he the man who brought the disease to America? "Dugas himself was infected by some other human, presumably during a sexual encounter—and not in Africa. Somewhere closer to home." As evidence now shows, HIV had already arrived in North America when Gaëtan Dugas was a virginal adolescent. "Using molecular genetics, researchers have now traced the exact strain of HIV that became a pandemic—HIV-1, Group M, Subtype B—to its original source. Amazingly, through examination of genetic samples from humans and chimps, Quammen reveals scientists have found exactly when and where AIDS started—even a probable theory as to how.[229]

Further research of HIV/AIDS can bring relief and a permanent solution to this disease that has ravaged the continent of Africa and beyond. It has, left marriages broken down, orphans devastated and hopeless, windows and widowers perplexed and in deeper sorrow and depression. The disease has caused unprecedented suffering for families, churches and communities, especially in Africa. Christ is the only answer and hope for those suffering from HIV/AIDS and other diseases. In biblical counseling, Christ stands out as the only hope, and every counselor must point the counselee to Jesus.

HIV/AIDS is active and needs to be dealt with now and in the future. Researchers continue to work through the solution to the complex disease that has claimed thousands of lives in Zimbabwe. Rose contends,

While condom use in Zimbabwe has been on the rise, a shortage of antiretroviral drugs, or ARVs, over the last 10 years has often meant HIV patients' access to such life-saving treatments has been sporadic, Avert reported. Developing an effective HIV vaccine is seen as the best way to end the global HIV/AIDS epidemic, which claims an estimated 1.5 million lives around the world every year.[230]

Research is taking place all over the world for a cure of HIV/AIDS. The hope is that the cure, a vaccine, and prevention will be found sooner rather later to stop the spread of the disease.

Theological Reflection

Theologically, the thesis has unveiled fundamental similarities between leprosy and HIV/AIDS in terms of stigma. Leprosy and HIV/AIDS have been treated with similar stigmatization. Leprosy bridges similar and relevant connection with HIV/AIDS in terms of human response. There are several lessons learned from the thesis. Leaders must love people genuinely and have compassion for them in their situations just as Christ demonstrated love. One cannot be a pastor and not love and have compassion for his congregation: "Greater love has no one than this that he lay down his life for his friends" (John 15:13 NIV). Christ gave a lesson to love people. HIV/AIDS church members deserve to be loved and equipped to live their lives fully and with purpose: "For equipping of the saints for the work of the ministry, for edifying of the body of Christ" (Eph. 4:12 NIV). Paul instructed Timothy to equip the body of Christ in Ephesus.

Christ showed the Israelites how to respond with love to the ten lepers who were regarded as outcasts (Luke 17:12-19 NIV). He embraced and accepted them into society. Christians and the church have an obligation to love and embrace church members with HIV/AIDS. Theological reflection on a biblical response to HIV/AIDS has impacted me in regard to the ministry of love, encouragement, giving, helping, and mercy demonstrated by the church and Christians. I learned significant lessons on how to relate to those stigmatized and shunned because of HIV/AIDS. Humbled by the servitude shown by the Lord Jesus Christ, I reflected on church leadership being portrayed today compared to Christ.

James challenges believers to be "But be doers" of the Word, and not hearers only, deceiving yourselves (James 1:22 NKJV). The "agape love," which is sacrificial love for others, demonstrated by Christ, must be emulated by all Christians. God's grace and faithfulness was experienced in the writing of the thesis. God's compassion, forgiveness, love, and reconciliation are the characteristics of God to His people. God came down to identify with his people's suffering and to rescue them from their bondage of sin. "The Lord said, 'I have indeed seen the misery of my people in Egypt. I have heard them crying out because of their slave drivers, and I am concerned about their suffering. So, I have come down to rescue'" (Exod. 3:7-8 NIV). Christ is "Emmanuel," God with us, who came to identify with people.

Personal Reflection

I learned three lessons in writing the thesis. First, God is the ultimate source of love, compassion, healing, and forgiveness. As the church engages people in counseling, the love of Christ must be demonstrated by action in through biblical counseling. I have a deep passion for HIV/AIDS positive people that have been shunned, especially by the church. It is my calling to bring the love and compassion of Christ to all those who are facing stigma. To write a biblical response to church members with HIV/AIDS was out of personal conviction to respond to such people. It has been enormously painful to see

HIV/AIDS positive people referred to physicians without receiving biblical counsel from the church. It is in that context in which a counseling institute was founded in Zimbabwe to counsel HIV/AIDS positive members of the church.

To achieve set goals, one has to have a strong team with the same vision and they must come together, without which nothing can be achieved. I have a gift of leadership; to draw and influence people to join me in achieving set goals. Through my leadership skills and experience in administration, I am able to draw people from different cultures and backgrounds. Forming and forging teamwork is one of my strengths. John C. Maxwell's *Developing Leadership within You* had a great influence on me. As Christ drew men to himself, a servant leader should be able to draw people in order to achieve goals through his character, leadership style, and humility.

People must be treated with dignity, mutual respect, and love, regardless of their condition, situation, race, or financial situation. In the eyes of God all people are equal, regardless of who they are or what their situations are. I learned that people who have HIV/AIDS often have suicidal thoughts because of depression. I became more understanding and developed a deeper comprehension of the impact of HIV/AIDS in the lives of people. I developed patience in dealing with HIV/AIDS people and how to better love and care for them. There was personal growth in learning how to counsel HIV/AIDS church members. The biblical research in this thesis strengthened my understanding of counseling HIV/AIDS church members and taught me how to better respond by imitating the way Christ responded to the lepers. The church must have the same attitude to those regarded as outcasts as the Lord Jesus Christ had toward lepers. I discovered that God's providence is amazing and His guidance to complete this thesis was truly His hand at work because it will help and guide Christian leaders to counsel their church members who have contracted HIV/AIDS. This thesis is a valuable tool that will go down in African church history as a way to deal with HIV/AIDS in the church and beyond.

Conclusion

The thesis was a great success in terms of addressing Christian leaders about counseling HIV/AIDS church members with a biblical response. The comparative analysis between leprosy in biblical Israel and HIV/AIDS in the twenty-first century brought insight to the church in how to counsel church members with HIV/AIDS. The role of the church to counsel and support members of the church with HIV/AIDS was explicitly discussed. The way the lepers in Israel were treated was discussed and practical examples from the Bible were discussed. The discussion brought to light how HIV/AIDS victims were treated during the first discovery of AIDS in Zimbabwe in the 1980s. The stigma of HIV/AIDS victims was similar stigma of lepers in Israel.

Preventative measures for HIV/AIDS were highlighted such as sexual behavioral change, sexual abstinence before marriage, and faithfulness within marriage, and the use of condoms for HIV/AIDS infected couples. Counseling children with HIV/AIDS, orphans, and women in African were highlights of the thesis. The practical response to HIV/AIDS gives the thesis relevance to the church and Christian leaders, and it gives Scripture a place in the twenty-first century church. The relevance of the practical solutions to HIV/AIDS allows the church to be actively involved in biblical counseling as a calling of the church at large.

BIBLIOGRAPHY

Books

Adams, Jay E. *Committed to Craftsmanship in Biblical Counseling.* Hackettstown, NJ: Timeless Text, 1994.

___. *Competent to Counsel*, Grand Rapid: Zondervan, 1990.

___. *Ready to Restore, Christian Counseling.* Phillipsburg, NJ: Presbyterian and Reformed, 1981.

___. *The Use of the Scriptures in Counseling.* Grand Rapids: Baker, 1975.

Allen, Clifton J. *Luke-John.* The Broadman Bible Commentary. Nashville: Broadman, 1970. Almond, Brenda. *Aids—A Moral Issue: The Ethical, Legal and Social Aspects.* New York: St. Martin's, 1990.

Amos, William. *When AIDS Comes to the Church.* Philadelphia: Westminster, 1988.

Anthony, E. James, and Colette Chiland, eds. *The Child in His Family.* New York: Wiley Interscience, 1988.

Anthony, Michael J., and James Estep, Jr. *Management Essentials Christian Ministries.* Nashville: B & H, 2005.

Becvar, S. Dorothy. *Soul Healing: A Spiritual Orientation in Counseling and Therapy.* New York: Harper Collins, 1997.

Berkley, James D. *Leadership Handbook of Management and Administration.* Grand Rapids: Baker, 1994.

Black, Matthew, and H. H. Rowley. *Peake's Commentary on the Bible.* London: Thomas Nelson and Son, 1962.

Blomberg, Craig L. *Matthew.* The New American Commentary, vol. 22. Nashville: Broadman, 1992.

Blumenfield, Warren J., and Alexander W. Scott. *AIDS and Your Religious Community: 27 Proven Models.* Boston: Unitarian Universalist Association, 1991.

Bock, Darrell L. *Luke.* The NIV Application Commentary. Grand Rapids: Zondervan, 1996.

Bourke, Hanson Dale. *Responding to HIV/AIDS.* Downers Grove, IL: IVP, 2013.

_____. *The Skeptic's Guide to the Global AIDS Crisis: Tough Questions and Direct Answers.* Waynesboro, GA: Authentic Media, 2004.

Brooks, James A. *Mark.* The New American Commentary, vol. 23. Nashville: Broadman, 1991.

Brueggemann, Walter. *1 & 2 Kings.* Smyth & Helwys Bible Commentary. Macon, GA: Smyth & Helwys, 2000.

Butter, George A. *Luke.* The Interpreter's Bible, vol. 2. New York: Abingdon, 1953.

___. *Luke.* The Interpreter's Bible, vol. 8. New York: Abingdon, 1952. Calvin. Jean. *Matthew, Mark, and Luke.* Commentary on Harmony of the Evangelists, vol. 3. Grand Rapids: Baker, 1996.

Capps, Donald. *Biblical Approaches to Pastoral Counseling.* Philadelphia: Westminster, 1981.

Carson, Donald A., T. France, Alec J. Motyer, and Gordon J. Wenham. *New Bible Commentary.* Leicester: Inter-Varsity, 1994.

Chaddock, Fred B. *Luke.* Interpretation. Louisville: John Knox, 1990.

Clare, Betty Moffatt. *When Some One You Love Has AIDS.* Santa Monica, CA: IBS, 1986

Connolly, Sean. *AIDS Pastoral Care: An Introductory Guide.* Grantsburg, WI: Arc Research, 1994.

Coyle J. Kevin, and Muir C. Steven. *Healing in Religion and Society: From Hippocrates to Puritans.* Lampeter, NY: Edwin Mellen, 1999.

Craddock, Fred B. *Luke.* Interpretation. Louisville: John Knox, 1973. Crowther, E. Colin. *AIDS: A Christian Handbook.* London: Epworth, 1991. Cummings, Ann Margaret. *Touched by AIDS.* Wheaton, IL: Tyndale, 1992.

Dhube, T. Joshua. *Celebrating 100 Years of Gospel Witness (1897-1997).* Harare, Zimbabwe: Jongwe, 1997.

Dortzbach, Deborah, and Meredith W. Long. *The AIDS Crisis: What We Can Do.* Downers Grove, IL: IVP, 2006.

Dube, Musa Wenkosi. *The HIV & AIDS Bible.* Scranton, PA: University of Scranton Press, 2008.

Edgar, Timothy, Anne Mary Fitzpatrick, and Vicki S. Freimuth. *AIDS: A Communication0 Perspective.* Hillsdale, NJ: Lawrence Erlbaum, 1992.

Elwell, Walter A. *Evangelical Commentary on the Bible.* Grand Rapids: Baker, 1989.

Everstine, Louis. *The Anatomy of Suicide: Silence of the Heart.* Springfield, IL: Charles C. Thomas, 1998.

Finzel, Hans. *The Top Ten Mistakes Leaders Make.* Colorado Springs, England: Victor, 1994.

Fitzgibbons, R. D. Enright. *Helping Clients Forgive: An Empirical Guide for Resolving Anger and Restoring Hope.* Washington, DC: American Psychological Association, 2000.

France, R. T. *The Gospel of Matthew*: New International Commentary to the New Testament. Grand Rapids: William B. Eerdmans, 2007.

Frumkin, Lyn Robert, and Leonard John Martin. *Questions & Answers on AIDS.* Oradell, NJ: Medical Economics Books, 1987.

Gardner, William, Susan G. Millstein, and Brian L. Wilcox. *Adolescents in the AIDS Epidemic.* San Francisco: Jossey-Bass, 1990.

George, Ricky L. *Counseling the Chemically Dependent: Theory and Practical.* Englewood Cliffs, NJ: Prentice Hall, 1990.

Gill, Robin. *Reflecting Theologically on AIDS: A Global Change.* London: SCM, 2007. Goldmann, R. David. *American College of Physicians: Complete Home Medical Guide.* New York: DK, 1999.

Gray, John. *1 &2 Kings: A Commentary.* 2nd ed. Philadelphia: Westminster, 1970.

Greenberg, S. Leslie. *Emotional Focused Therapy.* Washington, DC: American Psychological Association, 2002.

Grudem, Wayne, *Systematic Theology.* Grand Rapids: Intervarsity, 1994.

Hall, Jyl, Laura Barton, Michaela Dodd, Patrick James, and Jackie Yoshimura. *A Guide to Acting on AIDS. Understanding the Global AIDS Pandemic and Responding through Faith and Action.* Tyrone, GA: Authentic, 2006.

Hans, Finzel. *Change Is Like a Slinky.* Chicago: Northfield, 2004.

Hare, Douglas R. A. *Matthew.* Interpretation. Louisville: John Knox, 1993.

Hartley, John E. *Leviticus.* Word Biblical Commentary, vol. 4. Dallas: Word, 1992.

Hayes, Helen, and Cornelius Van der Poel. *Health Care Ministry*. New York: Paulist, 1990. Hoffman, Patricia L. *AIDS and the Sleeping Church: A Journal*. Grand Rapids: William B. Eerdmans, 1995.

Hoffman, Mary Ann. *Counseling Clients with HIV Disease*. New York: Guilford, 1996.

Hoffman, W. Wendell, and Stanley Grenz. *HIV/AIDS*. Grand Rapids: Baker, 1990.

House, Paul R. *1 & 2 Kings*. The New American Commentary, vol. 8. Grand Rapids: Broadman and Holman, 1995.

Jacobs, Douglas, and Herbert N. Brown. *Suicide: Understanding and Responding*. Madison, CT: International University Press, 1989.

Jager, Hans, ed. *AIDS and AIDS Risk Patient Care*. New York: Ellis Horwood, 1988.

Johnson, Eric, L. *Foundations for Soul Care: A Christian Psychology Proposal*. Downers Grove, IL: Intervarsity, 2007.

Johnson, Sheri L., Tiffany M. Field, Neil Schneiderman, Philip M. McCabe, Adele M. Hayes, and Lawrence Erlbaum. *Stress, Coping, and Depression*. Mahwah, NJ: Lawrence Erlbaum, 2000.

Just, Arthur A., Jr. *Luke*. Ancient Christian Commentary on Scripture New Testament, vol. 3. Downers Grove, IL: Intervarsity, 2003.

Kalipeni, Ezekiel, Karen Flynn, and Cynthia Pope. *Strong Women, Dangerous Times*. New York: Nova Science, 2009.

Kaplan, Singer Helen. *The Sexual Desire Disorders*. New York: Brunner/Mazel, 1995.

Kavar, F. Louis. *Pastoral Ministry in the AIDS Era: Focus on Families and Friends of Persons with AIDS*. Wayzata, MN: Woodland, 1988.

Klein, W. Ralph. *1 Samuel*. Word Biblical Commentary, vol. 10. Nashville: Thomas Nelson, 2000.

Kouzes, M. James, and Barry Z. Posner. *Christian Reflection on Leadership Challenge*. San Francisco: Jossey-Bass, 2004.

___. *Leadership Challenge*. 3rd ed. San Francisco: Jossey-Bass, 2003.

Leaney, A. R. C. *A Commentary on the Gospel according to St. Luke*. 2nd ed. London: Adam & Charles Black, 1966.

Leithart, Peter J. *I & II Kings*. Brazos Theological Commentary on the Bible. Grand Rapids: Brazos, 2006.

Liefeld, Walter, and David Pao. *Luke*. In vol. 10 of *The Expositor's Bible Commentary*. Edited by Tremper Longman III and David E. Garland, 268. Grand Rapids: Zondervan, 2007.

Luecke, David S., and Samuel Southhard. *Pastoral Administration: Integrating Ministry with and Management in the Church*. Waco, TX: Word, 1986.

MacArthur, John. *Romans 9-16. The MacArthur New Testament Commentary*. Chicago: Moody, 1994.

Malphurs, Aubrey. *Advanced Strategic Planning: A New Model for Church and Ministry Leaders*. Grand Rapids: Baker, 2000.

___. *Matthew*. In vol. 9 of *The Expositor's Bible Commentary*. Edited by Tremper, Longman III and David E. Garland, 25. Grand Rapids: Zondervan, 2010.

Maris, W. Ronald, Alan L. Berman, and Morton Silverman. *Comprehensive Textbook of Suicidology*. New York: Guilford, 2000.

Masters, H. William, Virginia E. Johnson, and Robert Kolodny. *Crisis: Heterosexual Behavior in the Age of AIDS*. New York: Grove, 1988.

Maxwell, C. John. *Developing the Leader within You*. Nashville: Nelson Business, 1993. Mays, James L. *The Harper Collins Bible Commentary*. San Francisco: HarperCollins, 2000. McConaghy, Nathaniel. *Sexual Behavior: Problems and Management*. New York: Plenum, 1913.

Morris, Leon. *Luke*. Tyndale New Testament Commentaries, vol. 3. Nottingham, England: InterVarsity, 1988.

Morris, L. Canon. *Luke: An Introduction and Commentary*. Grand Rapids: Intervarsity, 1988.

Nicolson, Ronald. *God in AIDS*. London: SCM, 1996.

Nolland, John. *Luke 1-9:20*. Word Biblical Commentary, vol. 35a. Dallas: Word, 1989.

Overberg, Kenneth R. *AIDS, Ethics, and Religion: Embracing a World of Suffering*. Mary Knoll, NY: Orbis, 1994.

Papdatou, Danai, and Costa Papadatos, eds. *Children and Death*. New York: Hemisphere, 1991.

Papolos, Demitri F., and Janice Papolos. *Overcoming Depression*. New York: Harper Perennial, 1992.

Patterson, Richard D., and Herman J. Austel. *1 Samuel*. In vol. 3 of *The Expositor's Bible Commentary*. Edited by Tremper Longman III and David E. Garland, 830. Grand Rapids: Zondervan, 2009.

Perelli, J. Robert. *Ministry to Persons with AIDS: A Family Systems Approach*. Augsburg, MN: Augsburg Fortress, 1991.

Plante, G. Thomas, and Allen C. Sherman. *Faith and Health: Psychological Perspectives*. New York: Guilford, 2001.

Plummer, Alfred. *A Critical and Exegetical Commentary on the Gospel*. Edinburgh: T & T, 1977.

Powers, Bruce P. *Church Administration Hand Book*. 3rd ed. Nashville: B & H, 2008.

ENDNOTES

1. Robin Gill, Reflecting Theologically on AIDS: A Global Change (London: SCM, 2007), 19.
2. Mary Ann Hoffman, Counseling Clients with HIV Disease (New York: Guilford, 1996), 7.
3. Brenda Almond, Aids: A Moral Issue (New York: St. Martin's, 1990), 26.
4. Shepherd Smith and Anita Moreland Smith, "Christians in the Age of AIDS," accessed May 2, 2012, http://www.allbookstores.com/Christians-Age- AIDS-Shepherd-Smith.
5. Ibid.
6. Avert.org, "HIV and AIDS in Zimbabwe," 1, accessed June 3, 2012, www.avert.org/aids-zimbabwe.htm.
7. Ibid., 4
8. Ibid.
9. Ibid., 5.
10. Avert.org, "HIV and AIDS in Zimbabwe," 5.
11. Lyn Robert Frumkin and John Martin Leonard, Questions & Answers on AIDS (Oradell, NJ: Medical Economics, 1987), 127.
12. D. A. Carson et al., The New Commentary (Leicester: Inter-Varsity, 1994), 63.
13. Hoffman, Counseling Clients with HIV Disease.
14. Almond, Aids—A Moral Issue.
15. William Amos, When AIDS Comes to the Church (Philadelphia: Westminster, 1988), 64.
16. Connolly Sean, AIDS Pastoral Care: An Introduction Guide (Grantsburg, WI: Sea Connolly, 1994), 4.
17. Musa Wenkosi Dube, The HIV & AIDS Bible (Scranton, PA: University of Scranton Press, 2008), 3.
18. Robert D. Enright and Richard P. Fitzgibbons, Helping Clients Forgive: An Empirical Guide for Resolving Anger and Restoring Hope (Washington, DC: American Psychological Association, 2000), 12.
19. Sheri L. Johnson et al., Stress, Coping, and Depression (Mahwah, NJ: Lawrence Erlbaum, 2000).
20. Patricia L. Hoffman, AIDS and the Sleeping Church (Grand Rapids: William B. Eerdmans, 1993), 46.
21. Ronald W. Maris, Alan L. Bernan, and Silverman Morton, Comprehensive Textbook of Suicidology (New York: Guilford, 2000), 34.
22. Robert J. Perelli, Ministry to Persons with AIDS: A Family Systems Approach (Augsburg, MN: Augsburg Fortress, 1991), 16.
23. Danai Papadatou and Costa Papadatos, eds., Children and Death (New York: Hemisphere, 1991), 11.
24. Nathaniel McConaghy, Sexual Behavior: Problems and Management (New York: Plenum, 1993), 3.
25. Letty M. Russell, The Church with AIDS: Renewal in the Midst of Crisis (Louisville: Westminster/John Knox, 1990), 12.
26. Gill, Reflecting Theologically on AIDS.
27. Jay E. Adams, Ready to Restore, Christian Counseling (Phillipsburg, NJ: Presbyterian and Reformed, 1981), 57.
28. Ibid.
29. Jay E. Adams, The Use of the Scriptures in Counseling (Grand Rapids: Baker, 1975), 28.
30. Ibid., 4
31. Adams, 5.
32. Jay E. Adams, "The Use of Scriptures," Bibliotheca Sacra 131, no. 552 (1974), 99-113.
33. Lyn Robert Frumkin and John Martin Leonard, Questions & Answers on AIDS (Oradell, NJ: Medical Economics, 1987), 12.
34. Ibid., 1/
35. John H. Sailhamer, Genesis, in vol. 1 of The Expositor's Bible Commentary, ed. Tremper Longman III and David E. Garland, rev. ed. (Grand Rapids: Zondervan, 2008), 93.
36. D. A. Carson et al., New Bible Commentary, vol. 1 (Leicester: Inter-Varsity, 1994), 63.
37. R. R. Reno, Genesis, Journal of Hebrew Scriptures, vol. 10 (Grand Rapids: Brazos, 2010), 95.
38. Eric L. Johnson, Foundations for Soul Care: A Christian Psychology Proposal (Downers Grove, IL: Intervarsity, 2007), 44.
39. Peter J. Liethart, I & II Kings, Brazos Theological Commentary on the Bible, vol. 2 (Grand Rapids: Brazos, 2006), 193.
40. George Arthur Buttrick, Leviticus, The Interpreter's Bible, vol. 2 (New York: Abingdon, 1993), 62.
41. Mark F. Rooker, Leviticus, The New American Commentary, vol. 3A (Nashville: Broadman & Holman, 2000), 191.
42. Richard B. Vinson, Luke, Smyth & Helwys Bible Commentary (Macon, GA: Smyth & Helwys, 2008), 545.
43. John E. Hartley, Leviticus, Word Biblical Commentary, vol. 4 (Dallas: Word, 1992), 191.
44. Ibid.

45 Buttrick, Leviticus, 62
46 Paul R. House, 1, 2 Kings, The New American Commentary, vol. 8. (Nashville: Broadman & Holman, 1995), 280.
47 Craig L. Blomberg, Matthew, The New American Commentary, vol. 22. (Nashville: Broadman, 1992), 138.
48 George Arthur Buttrick, Luke, The Interpreter's Bible, vol. 3 (New York: Abingdon, 1952), 298.
49 Fred B. Craddock, Luke, Interpretation: A Commentary for Teaching and Preaching (Louisville: John Knox, 1973), 203.
50 25Alfred Plummer, A Critical and Exegetical Commentary on the Gospel of St. Luke (Edinburgh: T & T, 1977), 402.
51 Robert H. Stein, Luke, The New American Commentary, vol. 24 (Nashville: Broadman, 1992). 434.
52 Darrell L. Bock, Luke, Encountering New Testament: A Historical and Theological Survey, vol. 2 (Grand Rapids: Bakers, 1996), 1399.
53 Ibid., 1400.
54 Darrell L. Bock, Luke, The NIV Application Commentary (Grand Rapids: Zondervan, 1996), 445.
55 Ibid., 446
56 A. R. C. Leaney, A Commentary on the Gospel According to St. Luke, 2nd ed. (London: Adam & Charles Black, 1966), 182.
57 Letty M. Russell, The Church with AIDS: Renewal in the Midst of Crisis (Louisville: Westminster/John Knox, 1990), 175.
58 Russell, The Church with AIDS, 33.
59 Ibid., 80
60 Russell, The Church with AIDS, 81.
61 Ibid., 160.
62 Frumkin and Leonard, Questions & Answers, 28.
63 Charlotte A Roberts, Mary, E. Lewis, and Manchester, K., The Past and Present of Leprosy (Oxford: Archae, 2002), 7.
64 Ibid.
65 Roberts, Lewis, and Manchester, The Past and Present of Leprosy, 7.
66 Donald Capps, Biblical Approaches to Pastoral Counseling (Philadelphia: Westminster, 1981), 20.
67 Ibid., 21
68 Ibid., 22
69 Jay E. Adams, Committed to Craftsmanship in Biblical Counseling (Hackettstown, NJ: Timeless Text, 1994), 21.
70 Frumkin and Leonard, Questions & Answers, 13.
71 Adams, "The Use of the Scriptures," 514.
72 American Heritage Dictionary, "Leprosy," accessed April 21, 2012, http://education.yahoo.com/reference/dictionary/entry/leprosy.
73 Medical Dictionary, "Leprosy," accessed April 21, 2012, http://www.yahoo.com commedical-dictionary.thefreedictionary.com/leprosy.
74 Sean Connolly, AIDS Pastoral Care: An Introductory Guide (Grantsburg, WI: Arc Research, 1994), 5.
75 R. T. France, The Gospel of Matthew, New International Commentary on the New Testament (Grand Rapids: William B. Eerdmans, 2007), 302.
76 Ibid., 305
77 Frumkin and Leonard, Questions and Answers, 127.
78 Ibid., 128.
79 Ibid., 306.
80 Ben Witherington III, Matthew, Smyth & Helwys Bible Commentary (Macon, GA: Smyth & Helwys, 2006), 177.
81 Blomberg, Matthew, 138.
82 Douglas R. A. Hare, Matthew, Interpretation (Louisville: John Knox, 1993),
83 Betty Clare Moffatt, When Some One You Love Has AIDS (Santa Monica, CA: IBS, 1986), 56.
84 Connolly, AIDS Pastoral Care, 23.
85 Musa Wenkosi Dube, The HIV & AIDS Bible (Scranton, PA: University of Scranton Press, 2008), 3-4.
86 Frumkin and Leonard, Questions & Answers, 3.
87 Dube, The HIV & AIDS Bible, 4.
88 Ibid., 123,
89 Dube, The HIV & AIDS Bible, 69.
90 James A. Brooks, Mark, The New American Commentary, vol. 23 (Nashville: Broadman, 1991), 137.
91 James A. Brooks, Mark, The New American Commentary, vol. 23 (Nashville: Broadman, 1991), 137.
92 World Council of Churches, Facing AIDS: The Challenge, the Church's Response (Geneva: WCC, 1997), 77.
93 World Council of Churches, Facing AIDS, 77.

94 John MacArthur, Romans 9-16, The MacArthur New Testament Commentary, vol. 10 (Chicago: Moody, 1994), 173.
95 David S. Luecke and Samuel Southhard, Pastoral Administration (Waco: Word, 1986), 108.
96 Luecke and Southhard, Pastoral Administration, 115.
97 Michael J. Anthony and James Estep, Jr., Management Essentials Christian Ministries (Nashville: B & H, 2005), 33.
98 Mary Ann Hoffman, Counseling Clients with HIV/AIDS (New York: Guilford, 1996), 1.
99 Ibid., 5
100 Wayne Grudem, Systematic Theology (Grand Rapids: Intervarsity, 1994), 1064.
101 Hoffman, Counseling Clients, 42.
102 John MacArthur, Ephesians, The MacArthur New Testament Commentary, vol. 1 (Chicago: Moody, 1986), 342.
103 MacArthur, Ephesians, 342.
104 Ronald Nicolson, God in AIDS (London: SCM, 1996), 201.
105 Nicolson, God in AIDS, 78.
106 Ibid., 79.
107 Robin Gill, Reflecting Theologically on AIDS: A Global Change (London: SCM, 2007), 19.
108 Nicolson, God in AIDS, 92.
109 Gill, Reflecting Theologically on AIDS, 22.
110 Ibid., 24.
111 Frumkin and Leonard, Questions & Answers, 127.
112 Ibid., 44.
113 Jyl Hall et al, A Guide to Acting on AIDS (Tyrone, GA: STI Distribution North America, 2006), 5.
114 UNICEF, "HIV/AIDS in Africa," 2, accessed June 1, 2012, http://siteresources.worldbank.org/INTAFRREGTOPHIVAIDS/Resources/WB_HIV-AIDS-AFA_2007-2011_Advance_Copy.pdf
115 National AIDS Council, "AIDS Zimbabwe," 7, accessed June 3, 2012, www.avert.org/aids-zimbabwe.htm.
116 Ibid., 4.
117 National AIDS Council, "AIDS Zimbabwe," 7.
118 Ibid.
119 Mary Ann Hoffman, Counseling Clients with HIV Disease (New York: Guilford, 1996), 1.
120 2Sheri L. Johnson and Adele M. Hayes, Stress, Coping and Depression (Mahwah, NJ: Lawrence Erlbaum Associates, 2000), ix.
121 Janice Wood Wetzel, Clinical Handbook of Depression (New York: Gardner, 1984), 1.
122 Wetzel, Clinical Handbook of Depression, 7.
123 Ibid., 9.
124 Hoffman, Counseling Clients with HIV Disease, 73
125 R. Ingalla and N. Oliver, "Depression Beater/ Understanding Depression," 12, accessed January 8, 2013, http://www.depressionbeater.com/Understanding-Depression,(2270954).htm.
126 Ibid.
127 R. Ingall and N. Oliver, "Depression—A Misunderstood Illness: Understanding and Treating Depression," accessed January 9, 2013, www.Depression- a Misunderstood Illness: Understanding and Treating Depression.
128
129 Demitri F. Papolos and Janice Papolos, Overcoming Depression (New York: Harper Perennial, 1992), 177.
130 Ibid. 249.
131 Kay Frances Schepp, Sexuality Counseling (Muncie, IN: Accelerated Development, 1986), 245.
132 Brenda Almond, AIDS-A Moral Issue: The Ethical, Legal and Social Aspects (New York: St. Martin, 1990), 33.
133 Ibid.
134 Ibid., 38.
135 Leslie S. Greenberg, Emotional Focused Therapy (Washington, DC: American Psychological Association, 2002), 256.
136 Greenberg, Emotional Focused Therapy, 261.
137 Dorothy S. Becvar, Soul Healing: A Spiritual Orientation in Counseling and Therapy (New York: Harper Collins, 1997), 48.
138 Avert.org, "HIV and AIDS in Zimbabwe," 1, accessed June 3, 2012, www.avert.org/aids-zimbabwe.htm.
139 Helen Land, A Complete Guide to Psychosocial Intervention (Milwaukee: Family Service America, 1992), 154.
140 Avert.org, "HIV and AIDS in Zimbabwe," 1.
141 Danai Papadatou and Costa Papadatos, eds., Children and Death (New York: Hemisphere, 1991), 3.
142 Ibid., 5.
143 Land, A Complete Guide, 154.
144 Papadatou and Papadatos, Children and Death, 4.
145 Papadatou and Papadatos, Children and Death, 102.

[146] Papadatou and Papadatos, Children and Death, 156.
[147] Ibid., 5.
[148] Land, A Complete Guide, 154.
[149] Musa Wenkosi Dube, The HIV & AIDS Bible (Chicago: University of Chicago Press, 2008), 103.
[150] Dube, The HIV & AIDS Bible, 155.
[151] Ezekiel Kalipeni, Karen Flynn, and Cynthia Pope, Strong Women, Dangerous Times (New York: Nova Science, 2009), 2.
[152] Almond, AIDS-A Moral Issue, 44.
[153] Ibid., 45.
[154] Almond, AIDS-A Moral Issue, 3.
[155] Ibid., 19.
[156] Susan L. Simonds, Depression and Women: An Integrative Treatment Approach (New York: Springer, 2001), 2.
[157] Adams, Critical Stages of Biblical Counseling, 36.
[158] Simonds, Depression and Women, 3.
[159] Ibid., 4.
[160] Ibid., 4
[161] Wetzel, Clinical Handbook of Depression, 50.
[162] Jay E. Adams, The Use of Scriptures in Counseling (Grand Rapids: Baker, 1975), 4.
[163] Simonds, Depression and Women, 14.
[164] Simonds, Depression and Women, 14.
[165] Douglas Jacobs and Herbert N. Brown, Suicide: Understanding and Responding (Madison, CT: International University Press, 1989), 6.
[166] Ibid., 13.
[167] Louis Everstine, The Anatomy of Suicide: Silence of the Heart (Springfield, WA: Charles C. Thomas, 1998), 20.
[168] Ibid., 21.
[169] Ibid., 23.
[170] Everstine, The Anatomy of Suicide, 24.
[171] Figure 5 taken from Everstine, The Anatomy of Suicide, 30
[172] Everstine, The Anatomy of Suicide, 31.
[173] Ibid.
[174] Alec Roy, Suicide (Baltimore: Williams and Wilkins, 1986), 5.
[175] Jay E. Adams, Competent to Counsel (Grand Rapid: Zondervan, 1990), 20.
[176] Ibid., 24.
[177] Ibid.
[178] Ronald Nicolson, God in AIDS? A Theological Enquiry (London: SCM, 1996), 88.
[179] Ibid., 82.
[180] Ibid., 85.
[181] Dale Hanson Bourke, Responding to HIV/AIDS (Downers Grove, IL: IVP, 2013), 75.
[182] Ibid. 76.
[183] James E. Anthony and Colette Chiland, The Child in His Family (New York: Wiley Interscience, 1988), 11.
[184] Ibid., 34.
[185] Bourke, Responding to HIV/AIDS, 77.
[186] Shirley C. Samuels, Disturbed Exceptional Children (New York: Human Science, 1981), 13.
[187] Ibid., 19.
[188] Samuels, Disturbed Exceptional Children, 26.
[189] Ibid.
[190] Hertha Riese, Heal the Hurt Child (Chicago: The University of Chicago Press, 1962), 30.
[191] Ibid., 34.
[192] Nicolson, God in AIDS?, 92
[193] See appendix 1.
[194] Mary Ann Hoffman, Counseling Clients with HIV Disease (New York: Guilford, 1996), 1.
[195] Hoffman, Counseling Clients, 2
[196] Michael Shernoff, Counseling Chemically Dependent People with HIV Illness (New York: Haworth, 1991), 17
[197] Hans Jager, AIDS and AIDS Risk Patient Care (New York: Ellis Horwood, 1988), 40.
[198] Ibid., 41
[199] Patricia L. Hoffman, AIDS and the Sleeping Church: A Journal (Grand Rapids: William B. Eerdmans, 1995), 46.
[200] Deborah Dortzbach and W. Meredith Long, The AIDS Crisis: What We Can Do (Downers Grove, IL: InterVarsity, 2006), 14.
[201] Ibid.

[202] Dortzbach and Long, The AIDS Crisis, 14.
[203] Hoffman, Counseling Clients, 47.
[204] Hoffman, Counseling Clients, 50.
[205] Lawrence E. Sullivan, Healing and Restoration: Health and Medicine in the World's Religious Traditions (New York: Macmillan, 1989), 248.
[206] Dortzbach and Long, The AIDS Crisis, 119.
[207] Dortzbach and Long, The AIDS Crisis...
[208] Ibid., 120.
[209] Musa Wenkosi Dube, The HIV/ AIDS Bible (Scranton, PA: University of Scranton Press, 2008), 173.
[210] Dube, The HIV/ AIDS Bible, 178.
[211] Shernoff, Counseling Chemically Dependent People, 135.
[212] Ibid., 137
[213] Sheri L. Johnson and Adele M. Hayes, Stress, Coping and Depression (Mahwah, NJ: Lawrence Erlbaum Associates, 2000), 297.
[214] Kevin J. Coyle and Steven C. Muir, Healing in Religion and Society from Hippocrates to the Puritans (Lewiston, NY: Edwin Mellen, 1999), 43:85.
[215] Earl E. Shelp and Ronald H Sunderland, AIDS and the Church (Louisville: Westminster/John Knox, 1992), 10.
[216] Ibid., 15.
[217] Margot Taller et al., HIV Positive: Perspective on Counseling (Philadelphia: The Charles Press, 1991), 30.
[218] Ibid., 5.
[219] Ibid., 11.
[220] Helen Hayes and Cornelius Van der Poel, Health Care Ministry (New York: Paulist, 1990), 10.
[221] Robert J. Perilli, Ministry to Persons with AIDS (Minneapolis: Augsburg Fortress, 1991), 13.
[222] Betty Clare Moffat, When Someone You Love Has AIDS (Los Angeles: IBS, 1986), 24.
[223] Louis F. Kavar, Pastoral Ministry in the AIDS Era: Focus on Families and Friends of Persons with AIDS (Wayzata, MN: Woodland, 1988), 20
[224] Ibid., 25.
[225] Bill Kirkpatrick, AIDS Sharing the Pain: Pastoral Guidelines (London: Darton, Longman and Todd, 1988), 4.
[226] Ibid., 5.
[227] Hoffman, Counseling Clients, 159.
[228] Allen E. Ivey, Norma Gluckstern, and Mary B. Ivey, Basic Attending, 3rd ed. (North Amherst, MA: Micro Training Association, 1997), 15.
[229] David Quammen, The Chimp and the River: How AIDS Emerged from the African Forest (New York: W. W. Norton and Company, 2015), 12.
[230] Quammen, The Chimp and the River, 12.

Printed by Libri Plureos GmbH in Hamburg, Germany